Presented To:

_____

From:

_____

Date:

_____

The
VICTORIOUS
Journey

CHIDI OSUJI

The
VICTORIOUS
Journey

CHIDI OSUJI

Published By Open Scroll Publications

Copyright © 2021 Chidi Osuji

First Edition by:
Open Scroll Publications Ltd,
Kemp House, 160 City Road,
London, EC1V 2NX.
www.openscroll.co.uk

ISBN:978-1-9999856-7-7

A CIP catalogue record for this book is available from the British library.

Edited by Diane Wilkie. Email: dee.wilkie7@hotmail.co.uk

Cover design and Typeset by Open Scroll Publications Ltd.

Printed in Great Britain.

Endorsements

This is a love story.

A love story between Charles and Chidi, as a I knew them. Even their names chime.

But it wasn't a frivolous, fleeting romance.

In the words of the Marriage Service, it was 'for better, for worse, for richer, for poorer, in sickness and in health, to love and to cherish 'till death do us part.'

This love story fulfilled all those promises.

It wasn't an exclusive love story either. Initially it embraced both sets of families and friends, but then it included their children and grandchildren. I knew them to the 'second' generation – Carol, Anthony and Fred – but rejoiced to read about the 'third' generation.

All of this would make the love story wonderful but there was more.

Much, much more.

God Himself was in this love story.

So, into the story come Bible promises, answered prayer, 'rhema' words, dreams (lots of them), spiritual warfare, fasting - plus laughter, joy, family feasts, peace in crisis, divine guidance and a home coming. "In my Father's house are many mansions...."

The love of the God, who is love, takes any love story to another level.

This one soars into heavenly places in Christ Jesus and walks through deep valleys.

It crosses continents.

Moves between hospitals and clinics and surgeries.

Changes churches.

(That's where I came in when they came to Walsall Evangelistic Centre, which became The Church at Junction 10.)

I am privileged to have had this love story touch my life.

I will be forever grateful for that!

And for them!

Pastor John H. Price

In THE VICTORIOUS JOURNEY, Chidinma has written the story of her life in a very unique style, that enables the reader to live her life with her, as if they were there in person. With her early childhood straddling across village and town life, and also embracing the scary experiences of the Nigerian civil war, the reader is taken step by step through her growing up, education and romance, that finally culminated in her marriage to her late husband.

Family life with the arrival of the children, and the very many changes in the family home and base, as they moved from Nigeria to the United Kingdom, is related with a clarity and vivacity that makes it difficult to put the book down. Through the varied and often extreme health challenges that confronted her family, the strong but practical day to day Christian faith, based on her commitment to the Lordship of Jesus Christ, cannot fail to challenge and inspire the reader.

Her strong character and the tenacity of her faith, stand out all the time and right to the end. The reader is also privileged to have a good view of the workings of a Christian family, the biblical way of raising children, and the balance and stability that such a close-knit Christian family brings to everyday life.

The book commends itself to the reader, and we count it a privilege ourselves, to recommend it as necessary reading for all of the family, parents and children alike.

Dr & Dr (Mrs) Nwachukwu James Nwabineli

Scripture tells us: *For everyone born of God overcomes the world. This is the victory that has overcome the world, even our faith* – 1 John 5:4

Chidi beautifully reveals in each page her love for the Lord, her reverence and total surrender to God. We see a life of prayer and unwavering faith, in the face of many challenges.

You will be taken through a journey of victory after victory, as we see God's love, direction and His absolute faithfulness! Indeed, our God is faithful.

Does God answer prayer! Is God still healing today? Read this book. It will encourage you through the inevitable storms of life. See God revealed in every page of this book, and the obedient response of a true warrior and child of God. Taste and see that the Lord is good!

Chidi – I have been so blessed to have spent three wonderful years with you at CBC. Thank you and God bless you for this book my beautiful Sister in Christ.

Milli Williams – Charis Bible College Graduate

Dedication

*I*n loving memory of my beloved husband (Charlie) Eze. I thank God for the thirty-nine years we shared together. Captured in faith, family and fun. Till we meet to part no more.

Preface

When the Lord invited me for a walk, I considered it an honour and a privilege that the Most High God would ask me to walk with Him. Although the invitation came in my adult life, God already chose me from before the foundation of the world.

A walk with God is not a walk in the park. It's a life long journey. Mine has been victorious and will remain so, because of what the Lord Jesus accomplished by His death, burial and glorious resurrection. As with every victory, there's first a fight; for there really is no victory without a fight. But we are assured of victory all the way, because of God's ever abiding presence.

In this book I have attempted to chronicle my victory reports, in the course of this lifelong walk, thus far. Right from my early years, when unknown to me, His steadfast, loving hands faithfully guided me in the path of destiny. This was oftentimes through the loving, dutiful and caring hands of parents and grannies. It became very clear to me that God had been beckoning and waiting for me to respond.

In this book, I have shared dreams, visions and words from the Lord, gleaned from times of fellowship with Him. These precious words have been the key to victory after victory, even at very obvious times of pain and conflict.

In this book, you will learn that my joy and dependency

is in Christ and Christ alone, and for this cause I faint not; because He is all sufficient. I have to mention that all parts of this book are based on true life experiences, recorded over the years. Victory comes when we let Jesus shine the way for us, as we depend on His word and not our circumstances. Let's look to Him, He knows the way.

God bless you.

The Lord is my light and my salvation;
Whom shall I fear?
The Lord is the strength of my life;
Of whom shall I be afraid?
² When the wicked came against me
To eat up my flesh,
My enemies and foes,
They stumbled and fell.
³ Though an army may encamp against me,
My heart shall not fear;
Though war may rise against me,
In this I will be confident.
⁴ One thing I have desired of the Lord,
That will I seek:
That I may dwell in the house of the Lord
All the days of my life,
To behold the beauty of the Lord,
And to inquire in His temple.
⁵ For in the time of trouble
He shall hide me in His pavilion;
In the secret place of His tabernacle
He shall hide me;
He shall set me high upon a rock.
And now my head shall be lifted up above my en-
emies all around me; Therefore I will offer sacri-
fices of joy in His tabernacle;
I will sing, yes, I will sing praises to the Lord.
⁷ Hear, O Lord, when I cry with my voice!
Have mercy also upon me, and answer me.
⁸ When You said, "Seek My face,"
My heart said to You, "Your face, Lord,
I will seek."

PSALM 27 Verses 1-8

Acknowledgements

I want to start by thanking my children, Uzoma, Ugo and Emeka. My daughters-in-law Cynthia and Bianca, My grandchildren Ella, Amarachi, Gabrielle and Brielle. You are my pride and joy and you mean the world to me. Tons of love.

To my extended family: (the Osuji and Atuonwu crew), I salute you all for your love and support throughout, especially at a very difficult time in my life. Thank you.

The Kabod Revival Ministries have literally held my hands through a great part my journey. From when I couldn't sing, to when I found my voice and could passionately sing again. I thank you immensely and I pray that your oil will never run dry.

To my Church family: (The Church at Junction Ten Walsall) I thank you for being there and doing what you do best.

To Charis Bible college Walsall and the entire World Out Reach of Andrew Wommack Ministries: A massive thank you for creating an environment that led to my healing. I was grief stricken when I started, but finished with a renewed and refreshed mind.

I really want to appreciate my brother Enyioma Buchi Atuonwu and my son Ugo Anthony Osuji, who proofread my manuscript and went the extra mile, at the expense of their own schedules. Also my brother Obinna Atuonwu, for helping me with some historic facts about our childhood. I love you all.

Sincere gratitude to Diane Wilkie who edited my manuscript, Pastor Michael Ekwulugo of Open Scroll Publishing for your patience, encouragement and excellent Work.

A big thanks to my nephew Marizu Ikechi Atuonwu, for designing the cover of my book. Thank you.

Sincere thanks to Robin Chellaswamy, who gave me Godly counsel about the editing of my manuscript at a time most needed.

I want to also appreciate my good friends who have stood by my family and I, through thick and thin. May the good Lord bless you more than you can think or imagine.

My ultimate thanks is to the most high God who told me to "write it down," and without whom I wouldn't be here today. I love you Lord. Thank you.

CONTENTS

Dedication 10

Preface 11

Psalm 27 13

Acknowledgments 14

Part 1

Chapter 1: House of Fun 21

Chapter 2: Experiencing War........................25

Chapter 3: The Hilly Campus 29

Chapter 4: Divine Orchestration.....................33

Part 2

Chapter 5: I Married My Best Friend................43

Chapter 6: Saved And Delivered......................49

Chapter 7: His Mercies Never Fail....................55

Chapter 8: God Has A Plan 61

Chapter 9: I Still Have Joy.............................69

Part 3

Chapter 10: Cast Your Eyes On Jesus.................77

Chapter 11: A Friend In Time Of Need............85

Chapter 12: Heeding The Call Of God.............89

Chapter 13: The Man I Call Charlie 99

Chapter 14: Saved By Grace 107

Chapter 15: I Was Troubled 115

Chapter 16: We Wrestle Not..............................129
            Against Flesh And Blood

Chapter 17: The Visitation.............................139

Chapter 18: The Glorious Exits 145

Chapter 19: God Is All Knowing 155

Chapter 20: My Charis Journey.....................161

Chapter 21: The Turning Point 167

Chapter 22: Mars Hill 175

Chapter 23: Reflections and Testimonies.......... 179

Chapter 24: God Is Our Refuge and strength 189

Chapter 25: Ebenezer...............................201

About The Author....................................209

PART 1

CHAPTER 1

HOUSE OF FUN

There is a beginning to every story and this one is no different. My story would not be complete without mentioning my childhood.

Growing up was fun and the memories will always remain with me. At the risk of sounding biased, I consider myself and my four brothers to have had the most amazing parents anyone could have wished for! I honestly pray my children will think the same of my husband and I.

In a house full of boys, life was all about football, male banter, endless laughter and of course lots of fights. I felt so blessed and they made me feel incredibly special. No one dared mess with me in the whole neighbourhood, because my brothers would sort them out straight away.

I remember returning home from school in Enugu one day, and some young boys mistakenly thought they could harass me and get away with it. Unbeknownst to them, two of my brothers were following and watching from afar. Suddenly when those rascals made a move to touch me, they honestly didn't know what hit them. They got much more than they bargained for, because my brothers taught them a good lesson. The poor lads learned that day, to never again harass any girl going about her business. They had no choice but to take to their heels! How protected I felt afterwards, and as proud as punch to have such loving and attentive brothers.

I remember fondly our Sunday specials. My mother was an excellent cook, second to none, if you ask me. It's as if the sun rises in my heart at every recollection of those sumptuous after-church meals. They were made all the more appetising by the expectation that preceded them, and the long wait all through the church service. The steamy hot rice and brownish red stew with juicy pieces of meat, jostling for your attention as they swam in the hot sauce, all seemed to call out to you as their vapour wafted through the air and hit your expectant nostrils... oh Sundays, they were my favourite!

My parents were God fearing, devout Christians and took their relationship with God very seriously. My mother was a 'lay-preacher,' in the Methodist church that we attended. This meant that, although she was not an ordained member of the clergy, she was still allowed to deliver sermons in church. She therefore served in that capacity, until she went home to be with the Lord.

My father was a chorister and played the accordion very well. His mother, my paternal grandmother, was a deaconess in the Apostolic Church. Dad would take me along to choir practices, and before long I joined in and it became second nature to me. Although I was the youngest member of the choir at age nine, I fitted right in and thoroughly enjoyed it. I have since sung in the choir or worship team, at every opportunity and wherever I found myself.

I stuttered badly as a child but ironically, it was singing that became an outlet for me. This was especially true whenever

I became angry and frustrated, at my inability to get my words out. This happened quite frequently, leading me to become the silent one in most group conversations, a frustration that found a means of release and solace in music. How the stuttering did not get in the way of my singing could only be by divine grace, and an actual miracle. Inevitably I was very reserved and quiet, always the one to observe everyone else and take note of things in my mind.

I remember this particular occasion during a big church event. It was packed with elites and distinguished personalities of high society. During the service as we were singing our hearts out, I was asked to do a bible recitation of the *twenty-third Psalm,* as well as another portion of scripture, from the *book of Isaiah* which I can't remember now.

Half way through the recitation something extraordinary happened. I suddenly drifted into a vision, where I could see angels and bright lights all around. I became so caught up in what I could see, that I was completely unaware of my physical environment, including how the exercise progressed, and how long it lasted.

When I did snap out of it and managed to recollect myself, all I could hear was thunderous applause for my recitation. At first I was sore afraid and thought perhaps I'd failed badly, until the young lady by my side told me how beautiful my recitation was. Now that got me confused, because I wasn't even aware of what I had been saying! All I knew was that God had given me a vision of angels and that's all I could honestly remember. I learned something that day. I was 'in the spirit,' and God took care of the rest.

My father was very proud of me and told me so as we

walked home. He was full of compliments about my recitation. I kept my little secret of what the Lord had shown me to myself, because I didn't know how to explain it to my dad, especially as I was still trying to understand it myself.

On another occasion however, I did share about my experience with the lady who had been at my side that day. She explained and acknowledged that the Lord had given me a vision! This became a treasure that I hid in the field of my heart as I grew up. I had other similar experiences, some of which will be mentioned later on in this book.

CHAPTER 2

EXPERIENCING WAR

In 1967 life changed as we knew it, as the Biafra civil war broke out in Nigeria. Most people fled for safety to their villages or hometowns. Civil servants had to be redeployed to the nearest headquarters, so my parents had to take us all back to the village, Ntalakwu Oboro in Ikwuano local Government in Abia State. This was part of the then Eastern Nigeria.

It was difficult to have to adapt to life in the village. School was a particular challenge as we found ourselves at the mercy of the local champions. They saw us 'returnees,' as some kind of greenhorns and seemed to relish trying to make things even more difficult for us. Thankfully however, our young uncle Emenike, was the Ebenezer who came to our rescue. He showed us the ropes and soon enough, we were able to stick up for ourselves.

Life was tough because of the war, made more so by the fact that my dad was miles away. He had to work at the nearest headquarters in Mbaise, while we stayed at home with my mother (lovingly called Mma) and our grandmother, fondly called Daa, and lots of uncles, aunties and cousins. Life changed as we became acquainted with their idea of fun, farming, snail hunting, swimming, and once again, I joined the church choir.

It was during this time that I had to learn to read, write and speak my native dialect of Igbo. I remember one occasion when my mother travelled to visit my father, and she had to be away for a few days so we stayed with Daa (grandma). One fateful day, my four brothers and I had gone out to play. My youngest brother Osondu, was only a toddler at the time. Part of the fun for us kids, was to swing on a weak palm branch which hung loose from the bunch. It rested invitingly on the trunk of the coconut palm, and being pushed by other kids made it into a swing and one of our most entertaining pastimes.

I left Osondu to his own devices and went to have my turn on the swing. Unfortunately this didn't go well as it turned out to be an ill-fated adventure. The palm branch suddenly snapped and detached itself while I was still mid-air, and I crash landed and lost consciousness for a few minutes. Even though I came out of it largely unhurt, the aches and pains that followed were enough for a life-long lesson! Needless to add that my grandmother's massage was more punitive than therapeutic. Miraculously, there were no after scars or delayed effects from the fall. I have God to praise for that.

Talking about miracles, I experienced another notable one during this war period and it was a very close shave. I was unwell with malaria, and felt so ill that I was lying on a long mud-built bed, while waiting for food and medicine to be served. Suddenly without warning I heard what was the most horrifying sound I had ever heard in my life! An airplane had been shot down and it was crash landing, brushing roof and trees tops and destroying everything along its path!

There was a lot of commotion and pandemonium. People were crying and screaming "take cover, take cover," as they ran helter-skelter. Soon afterwards I was left alone on that mud bed, as the plane went past with smoke billowing from out of one of its wings. I had no energy to run, so I just laid down there and watched. The plane eventually crashed at the nearby secondary school, causing indescribable devastation, but only to the school building! It was a Saturday so there was no one actually present at the school, when the plane crashed and burst into flames.

Again, God saved my life!

My mother was a very prominent woman, and as a teacher, she was involved in many community events and church activities. She was notably instrumental, to the running of the Girls Guide and Brownies in the community. I was one of the Brownies and always wore my uniform with so much pride.

In her Girls Guide-Brownies leader role, mother was assigned to assist with relief supplies, for the war-affected families which came from all over. I had to learn to walk miles on various errands, to either deliver or receive relevant messages. There were no telephones in those days, as the war had damaged the few telecommunication lines that existed at the time.

Finally in late 1969 the war ended and we returned to Enugu, at the beginning of 1970. The devastating effects of the war could be seen wherever you turned. Although my immediate family didn't suffer any casualty, or the dire starvation that characterised the actual war, the last two weeks of the war were profoundly traumatic for a child my age. At age eleven going on twelve, as the war was ending, it was most distressing to see dead bodies lying about. It was especially traumatic, as these were people we knew who wouldn't surrender, or were perceived as being resistant to the seat of power.

CHAPTER 3

THE HILLY CAMPUS

After the war, it took quite some time for some normalcy to return. It did to some extent, so two years later I was in secondary school and these were fun filled days.

Life was strict in the boarding school system of the Methodist Girls' Secondary School Ovim. It was situated on a hill and within walking distance from the train station.

I remember the morning runs which began at 5 am, fetching of water from the stream, first for your school mother, and then for yourself. (A school mother was an older student who was in a senior year and took you under her wing and looked after you. You then did little jobs and favours for her, especially when she was busy studying, and didn't always have time for practical chores).

In spite of this awful tasking semi-military regiment, if you were late for any activity, you were subjected to having to cut the grass on the expansive lawns, with nothing more than your cutlass.

The sporting events and some other programs of activities, organised periodically under the Religious Society, Science Club and Debating Society were the little fun we had. It was hardly enough for us, so I joined the school choir as well, and that was also quite some fun, with all the rehearsals and singing events.

During this time I had a dream. A man in a white robe came to me by the pool and gave me three passages from the book of **Psalms**, and told me that if ever I was in trouble, I was to recite them and pray using them, an exercise which has helped me all through my life so far. They were **Psalm 121, Psalm 34**, but I forgot the third one.

I also remember walking into the classroom one cool breezy evening, and hearing someone call my name. There was however no one else physically there. The voice instructed me to read the book of **Isaiah, chapter 61,** and this happened to me twice. These somewhat mysterious spiritual encounters, served to reassure me of the enduring guidance of the omnipresent God. It is such a great feeling to realise again and again, that God has been with me and is so mindful of me.

Boarding school was quite an experience. It offered us young ladies, our earliest practical lessons including economic management, as we had to learn to manage our pocket money. We also learned how to take care of our personal hygiene, to eat right and make do with the available cafeteria food. Also stocking up on back-up food provision proved to be the beginning of economic wisdom. This meant having a supply of Cabin biscuits and butter, your garri flour made from the Cassava plant (to be soaked in cold water), often with milk, sugar and Ovaltine (a cocoa beverage).

In a sense, they were not just backup items to augment the mostly miserable cafeteria food, but also substitute delicacies to be relished on the side. Cafeteria food never seemed to be enough, or good enough, that is until the term advanced into the second or third month. At this crucial time, when pocket money and food backups had run low or fizzled out, cafeteria food became curiously delicious again and in high demand! Those delicacies then became the objects of our fantasies. Only in our dreams and imaginations would we relish the comfort of garri soaked in a mixture of water, milk and sugar, or the sweet memories of arriving at the train station and rushing to the bukka (road-side restaurant) popularly known as, 'Mama Put,' for a plate of hot rice. Living at the boarding house certainly offered us, among other things, our earliest shot at resource management.

One of the major highlights of my secondary school was getting confirmed in church, and being prepared for the Holy communion. We had to learn and understand what Holy communion meant and the benefits of it. We even had to pass an exam first, and if successful, then we were allowed to get confirmed. It was a big milestone for us, and I remember the immaculate white dress, and well-polished shoes or sandals in which the new communicants had to appear in. The Methodist hymns will stay with me for the rest of my life!

Particularly fascinating to me was the history behind some of the hymns, especially those written by John and Charles Wesley, (two brothers who stood out among other greats) and of whom my parents often spoke of, with such great admiration and reverence.

I remember our sing song events and recitations. Looking back now, apart from being a rich manure for my latter-day love for music, it was a lot of fun, and lifelong friendships were forged.

Glorious memories!

CHAPTER 4

DIVINE ORCHESTRATION

When I completed secondary school in 1976, I headed back to Enugu where my parents lived and was faced with the news of another relocation. This time it was to a place called Owerri, another South Eastern city. The Nigerian government had split up the regions into several smaller unit states, so civil servants were required to move to their states of origin.

Until all the arrangements were finalized, my dad had to commute to Owerri to work, and would come back home to Enugu for the weekend. One day as he was travelling to work he met his good old friend, Chief R.E.D Osuji, popularly known as Red Duncan. This meeting became significant in more ways than one, especially as he later on became my father-in-law.

During their chat, my dad hinted that he was looking for a place to rent, which would ease the burden of commuting from Enugu to Owerri and having to run two homes.

Chief Osuji being a native, kindly offered my dad his house in the village straight away without hesitation. He and his family were not resident there, so the house was empty. This was very welcome news for our family so before long, off we moved to Nekede near Owerri. In a way, it was like moving back to the village again, although this turned out to be different.

This coincided with it being time for me to sit for the entrance examinations, to get into university and to pursue my dream career which was Journalism, with some training in Agriculture as a backup. One day, my father sat me down and asked what I really wanted to do with my life, so it was an opportunity to share my dreams with him. He listened to what I had to say, and then mentioned that my intentions were good. He did however feel strongly that I would be a good nurse, especially because of the qualities he'd seen in me as a father, and he left me with that thought. The rest as they say is history, as after much thought, I followed my father's advice. I have no regrets, nor have I looked back since.

As the long vacation came around, there were many students around in the village. I didn't really mingle that much because I was a home bird at heart. I did however still manage to quickly make friends, with other people my own age, who were also waiting for their West African School Certificate or Higher School results (as it was called in Nigeria back then), the prerequisite for admission to tertiary institutions.

At the same time Chief Osuji's eldest son, Etofolam Felix Osuji, came back home to his dad's house where we were living, to be based there while he did his internship, in one of the nearby organisations in the city.

Having him around was great as he was like an older brother, showing us round the village, and protecting us from people who would have ordinarily taken advantage of us. One day I remember sitting with my new friends, when someone that looked like Felix walked into our midst. Everyone else knew him except my friend Charity and I. It was all laughter and felicitation as one of his cousins introduced him to us. That young man was Charles Eze Osuji. He was popularly known as Charlie. Sometimes I fondly called him Charlie, and at other times I called him Eze.

Living as a tenant with my parents in his father's house, meant that I saw him each time he came to the village. He treated us much the same way his elder brother treated my brothers and I. We were like family, and because we had a lot in common, there was always much to talk about. He too had just completed high school education, and was awaiting his results. During this time we had many more people around the house, as his friends came round each time he was home. It wasn't long though however, before he went back to where his parents lived. (Chief Osuji and his wife, Charlie's parents, were both Nurses. An interesting coincidence, you might say. They were also easy going and caring people).

By September 1976 I gained admission to study Community Midwifery. I was heading to the school of Health Technology in Aba, to start my Nursing and Midwifery career. As a result of the earlier chat I'd had with my dad, I didn't manage to apply for my Nurse training in time, to get into any of the universities for Nursing. This is how I ended up doing my Midwifery at the School of Health Technology Aba, and my general Nursing training at Holy Rosary Hospital Emekuku, Owerri.

Initially Charlie wrote to tell me he had gained admission, to study Medicine at the University of Ibadan. We continued to exchange letters for a few months and after a good while, I noticed his letters were becoming interesting and a lot more frequent. Suddenly one day he just came out with it.

He fancied me and would like us to become more that casual friends. As it happened, I had begun to have thoughts I had never had before, a sure indication he could be 'the one!'

He was a great letter writer, keeping up communication between us even though we were hundreds of miles apart, and only able to see each other during vacations. Till then, getting his letters were the highlight of my day!

My parents had moved to the city during this time, while his parents moved back to their house in the village, that they had allowed us to live in as tenants. Sometimes Charlie spent his holidays in Warri where his sister lived with her family.

Life was great and I obviously didn't tell any of my folks, but it didn't take long for them to figure things out. My parents were very strict and austere, when it came to us kids having a social life, so there were no late nights or clubbing, though I wasn't particularly so inclined anyway.

I loved dancing and would dance to any music even radio and TV advertisements. At weekends as a student midwife, we went out to parties and it was all clean fun. When we had danced to our hearts content, we all returned to the campus before the gates were shut. One day however the happy-go-lucky group of social adventurers, got back to the campus later than usual… and later than the school allowed! Unfortunately for us, the gateman sure enough was there in his little cubicle, doing his work by keeping watch. If caught at this time, we would be sanctioned. *How in the world would my parents receive the news that I went to a dance party at that time of night? Scandalous!* I thought.

Scaling over the wall appeared to be the only option left and as such, we all climbed over the fence, a stone-throw from the gateman's cubicle. We could hear him shouting in a mixture of enquiry and alarm, "who's there?"

No one paid any attention to him as we managed to climb over the fence, and hide behind the shrubs in the compound. All but one girl made it over successfully. As she tried to get over, she fell as she tried to jump into the compound, and her dress got tangled in the flowers and ripped. Thankfully for her, the old gateman who was hysterical by now, was unable to catch up with her as we all fled to our hostel. It was such a close shave, and that naughty adventure was as far as we could take our truancy in those days. Looking back, that was clean and innocent fun, which pales in magnitude compared to the way things are today!

When we weren't invited to any parties, we entertained ourselves and were enraptured by watching the late night movies, usually slotted at 10:10pm by the Nigerian Television Authority. It became our habit to sit around in the Common Room and watch them together.

We also went bike riding, played football and participated actively in the Debating Society. There were also Scripture Union events, and crusades on campus that we took part in. I attended and listened but didn't go up for any altar calls. My Christian upbringing never left me however, as I always read my bible and prayed daily.

My relationship with Charlie was flourishing and quite solid at this time, and we both knew where we were headed, even though we were still miles apart. Indeed, the distance made it even more special as there was so much to talk about in our letters, or whenever we did manage to meet during the holidays.

When I turned 21 years old I graduated as a midwife and was posted to a very remote village, called Ebem Ohafia. Meanwhile, just before I graduated, Charlie asked me to be the mother of his children and to grow old with him, and I said YES!

Once I accepted his proposal, it was time to go public and let our parents know. He had no problems getting his parents' consent. When he came to see my parents, however it was a little less straight forward. They asked him to go away and think about his proposal carefully, because we were both young. Besides they would want me to get married to someone closer to my hometown as a preference. Nekede Owerri was considered to be too distant from Ikwuano Umuahia! I thought that was bizzare.

Although they loved him as a person, and wanted the family friendship that had spanned years to continue, the perceived distance between our hometowns (which by the way were in the same Imo State), threatened to become a clog in the wheel.

We carried on seeing each other when we could, although his parents had advised him to choose someone else, since my parents wouldn't give their blessing. My brothers came to visit and took turns to stay with me. My aunt who was on maternity leave also spent a long time with me, and so did my uncle, Prosper. He was posted there as an agriculturist to do his internship in Forestation.

The way things turned out with my parents' response to Charlie's proposal, left me feeling disappointed and sad. I went into a mood and refused to go back home, except when it was absolutely necessary. Coupled with the fact that the health centre where I worked was very busy, everything took so much effort. The drag continued, and after a while it all got a bit much, and Charlie and I decided to part ways. It was sad, painful and difficult. I was not interested in seeing anyone else.

Thankfully though the separation was short lived. After a few months, Charlie came to see me. He asked if I was dating anyone else, because he wasn't coping well with the separation. From that moment on, our relationship kind of continued; it never really stopped. When we split up, even though we had both agreed to go our separate ways, we had remained on the front burner of each other's heart and thoughts. Getting back together then was the most natural thing ever.

Perhaps my parents meant well trying to be protective of their only daughter, but our burning young hearts could neither understand nor excuse their stoic stand. I was particularly disappointed with my father's primitive consideration of distance between our hometowns. *How could this be a determination of our future together?* I wondered. *It was cruel and crushing,* I thought.

The time came when I had to go back to school for further studies in General Nursing. As part of the training, we were required to go for a Psychiatric posting for a period of time. During this time my mother came to the school to visit me, and I was very happy to see her. After her short stay, she said, "Ask Charlie to come to the house to see us, because I know that you still see each other."

I wasn't going to deny it so I kept quiet, pondering the rationale for her comment, and where she was going with it. As soon as I got the chance, I went ahead and relayed the message to Charlie. He asked me too many questions which I had no answers to.

He was a great letter writer, keeping up communication between us even though we were hundreds of miles apart, and only able to see each other during vacations. Till then, getting his letters were the highlight of my day!

PART 2

CHAPTER 5

I MARRIED MY BEST FRIEND

The arrangements were made and eventually Charles paid my parents a visit and, bravo! He got the nod as my parents finally gave us their blessings. Our joy and excitement knew no bounds. Now nothing was going to stop us! However they did put a slight spanner in the works. Typically, they asked me to take the necessary steps to get married slowly, to give me adequate time to finish my General Nurse training first.

In spite of my excitement, I couldn't help wondering what made my parents change their minds, after four whole years of solid resistance. During one of my weekend trips home, 'Mama Ukwu' my maternal grandmother, called me aside and told me exactly what had happened. " I sat your mother down and we had a chat about things," she admitted.

"I asked her why she wouldn't let you get married to the one you loved, just because of distance and cultural differences. I also reminded her that if I had listened to what people said to me, during her courtship days, then she wouldn't have married her husband!" It must have brought back memories, as it seemed to do the trick, she said grinning.

That intervention was quite sobering and helped me see why they eventually re-thought their position, and consequently gave us their blessing in the end. I will forever remember my maternal grandmother for that, and all the many other things she did. When she passed on, Charlie and I had to be there to celebrate her life with my family. She was much loved for her no-nonsense approach to life, hard work and resilience, not to mention what an excellent cook she was!

At that time recognition as a Midwife and General trained Nurse, was strictly by qualification, and as such it was a thing of great honour and high esteem. It was with joy and pride that we wore the purple belt over our white uniform.

Charlie had graduated as a doctor and completed his National youth service corps scheme, round about the same time that I finished my General Nursing training. As a staff nurse and midwife, I was posted to another remote village in Arochukwu. In the meantime our wedding preparations were well underway. We completed the traditional marriage rites in November1983 and we were right in the midst of our dream. Our love had prevailed, our patience and determination had paid off, and this was our dream becoming reality!

In a manner of speaking, the wedding was a trophy of triumph for us. We had our 'White wedding,' at Assumpta Cathedral Owerri on the 3rd of March 1984. It was the most beautiful day ever, and the church hall was packed with guests. I married my best friend, the love of my life, my confidant, after eight years of courtship.

Shortly after our wedding, we went on a trip to Jos, Plateau State where I was born, and a few miles away from Barkin Ladi where Charlie was born. It was great to spend some time there, enjoying the autumnal weather and a variety of choice food. As we travelled on our way, I felt sick as I was expecting our first child at this time. To try and cheer me up and to make fun out of the situation, Charlie gave me a carrier bag to relieve myself! I was most unimpressed and didn't find it funny at all.

On our way back from the trip, he had some food from one of the road side (bukkas), and few hours later he was desperate for the toilet. I handed him the same bag he gave me to relieve myself, to do his business! Needless to say he didn't find that funny, but thankfully it was almost time for the bus to stop for passengers to go for comfort breaks.

We always reflected on that trip and laughed about it. We concluded that its best to mind what you wish for regarding others, and how you handle distress, because you don't know what's round the corner for you to have to deal with.

Life was full of fun, laughter and so much joy. Soon, our first child arrived and we called her Uzoma Carol. (Uzoma meaning a good path and Carol is the feminine version of Charles). When I was pregnant with her, I had a dream. In the dream I was carrying a baby and my dad came to visit and said to me, "my child resembles my child." When I woke up, I realised that the baby would be a baby girl.

In those days there were no scans in the mid-Eighties, to give you an idea of the gender of your baby, so with the hint from my dream, we started shopping for girlie things and when she arrived, we were not disappointed. The excitement was very palpable in both families. Almost two years later, our second child Ugochukwu (God's eagle) Anthony arrived. In fact he arrived a very hungry baby, so we had to put him straight on a feeding bottle hours later, because it took a whole day for me to begin lactating properly.

Like with his sister, I also had a dream during my pregnancy with him. In that dream I was lying on what seemed like a hospital bed in a ward setting. A young man in a long white flowing dress walked in with a white bird, which I will describe as a dove in his hands. Shortly afterwards another man walked in with a pot on his head, with open flames of fire in it. He immediately wanted to fight the man in the white robe.

The man in the white robe, placed the white dove on to my bulging tummy and asked me to look after it. He turned round and began to fight the man with the pot of fire on his head. I was praying so hard that he would defeat the man with the fire on his head and he did. After that he turned round and collected the white dove from me, and left, then I woke up. That was a sign of victory, if you ask me.

A few months later our first son arrived. *He is the spitting image of Charlie*, I thought to myself. He was a big baby and whenever a visitor picked him up, they tended to hand him back after a few minutes because he was heavy. He was a big bouncing baby boy and such a joy to us.

Nine months later, Charlie decided to go back to university to specialise in Obstetrics and Gynaecology, at the University of Benin Teaching Hospital. We were going to live on just his basic salary, without other allowances. We knew it was going to be tight for the few years ahead, but we did not envisage the magnitude of challenges we were about to face.

We left the Okigwe General Hospital where he worked, and

moved to Owerri to stay with my parents, so they could help us with child care and support, while we found a suitable place for us to live in.

Another reason we had to leave Okigwe was because the accommodation was allocated to Charlie, as a hospital member of staff. I worked with the child health clinic which was under a different establishment.

My parents were now retired but mum had a small restaurant, which turned out to be a place of ministry, rather than a money-making venture.

Dad was always available to help me with errands, while doing his own accounting work, where he volunteered to help other people. For the next six years we were running two homes, but thank God for the gift of family. My parents were there to help and so was my brother in-law Lawrence Osuji (Charlie's younger brother). He was a medical doctor, though in private practice. He dropped by almost on a daily basis, to bring us stuff from his place of practice.

Just as Charlie went to study, I also decided to go back for further studies also. I had secured admission into the School of Public Health Nursing, to train as a public health nurse. It was really tough as I was juggling having a family, with studying, and coping with having a husband hundreds of miles away.

In 1987 I passed my West African Board Exams and graduated with a distinction, the first of its kind in the state. That made us happy and it goes to prove that with hard work you can achieve anything you want to! I will forever be grateful to my parents and brother in-law Lawrence, for all their support at that time.

But if we walk in the light, as he is in the light, we have fellowship one with another, and the blood of Jesus Christ his son cleanses us from all sin. If we say we have no sin, we deceive ourselves, and the truth is not in us. If we confess our sins, he is faithful and just to forgive us our sins and to cleanse us from all unrighteousness.
1John1:7-9

CHAPTER 6

SAVED AND DELIVERED

Shortly after my graduation, our third child was on the way. Having taken a study leave for my training, it was time to return to work. I had to commute about forty five miles daily, to go to work using public transportation. This was a huge challenge, because the roads were bad. It wasn't long before this started to affect my health, and I began to bleed, and feared for my unborn child. I knew I needed to rest but things were so hectic at work, and I felt pressured to go in every day. My mother suggested I stay with friends at Okigwe, once or twice a week, instead of commuting every day. She promised to take care of the children while I was away. I thought it was a good idea and took her advice.

During one of these trips I stayed with my friend Stella. We got chatting about faith and the Full Gospel Business Men's fellowship. Charlie was Catholic and after our wedding, we carried on attending the Catholic church which wasn't familiar to me, but I had to make the sacrifice because of our marriage.

I loved God and attended church regularly, read my bible and prayed on a daily basis. I had been invited to the Full Gospel fellowship a few times before, and loved attending the meetings but I wasn't born again yet. One day, my friend Stella was going to work on a late shift, so she gave me her note from a Full Gospel meeting to read.

As I sat alone in the house that day in quietness of the room, I read Stella's notes and the words went straight to my heart. Tears rolled down my cheeks as I wept bitterly. I remember asking myself, *why have you wasted so much time before surrendering yourself to Jesus?* I was overwhelmed by the Holy spirit, and confessed my sins before God. There and then, I gave my life to Jesus.

The scripture says in *1 John 1:7-9:*

> *But if we walk in the light, as he is in the light, we have fellowship one with another, and the blood of Jesus Christ his son cleanses us from all sin. If we say we have no sin, we deceive ourselves, and the truth is not in us. If we confess our sins, he is faithful and just to forgive us our sins and to cleanse us from all unrighteousness.*
> 1John1:7-9

I felt a weight lifted off my shoulders. There was abundant joy in my heart, but with a little sting of regret, that it had taken me so long to get to this point. Well there's no doubt that I had indeed wasted some time, but as we know, it's never too late to give your life to Jesus. I'm so glad I did. When my friend came back from work, I told her what had happened to me, and she joyfully prayed for me.

The next day, I was back in Owerri. I knew it wasn't going to be easy, but I also knew that Jesus would be with me every step of the way. I told my youngest brother Osondu (who was already a born again Christian), about it and he was very excited.

A few weeks later I noticed I was no longer stuttering! Oh the joy! I also realised that I didn't get angry so easily, and it took a lot more to make me feel angry. Interestingly, another curious thing was that whenever I did get angry, I got sick afterwards. I immediately resolved to put anger away from me for good. You see, Jesus didn't just save me that day, he also delivered me from severe anger and stammering. Praise God!!

When Charlie came home I shared my experience with him. He noticed straight away that something had changed about me, and he was happy for me. I encouraged him to give his life to Jesus also, but like water off a duck's back, my nudge was of no significance. When I stopped to think about it however, I became more in love with my husband, especially as I considered that he loved me regardless of the speech impediment and anger issues, that were flaws that had affected me.

As Charlie didn't yet share my faith, I began to struggle spiritually as a result. I still continued worshiping at the catholic church, but I wasn't being fed with the Word of God and it bothered me. I did all I could to quench the hunger in me, by reading my bible and praying all the time. I also began to tithe. When I started to pay tithes, they told me that they didn't know anything about such doctrine, but it didn't put me off or stop me. (I should point out, that this is not in any way a criticism of the catholic church, but simply my experience at the time).

On many occasions my hunger for the word of God led me to attend the Full Gospel Business Fellowship meetings, at the chapter close to me. I had a work colleague who was a strong scripture union member, and she eventually became my spiritual mentor.

Unfortunately as my pregnancy progressed, I started to have premature contractions because I was still commuting. I had to go to hospital and was immediately placed on bed rest. I remember praying and vowing to the Lord that if he delivered me from this ordeal, and protected my baby to full term, that he or she would serve the Lord.

Following shortly afterwards, I had a dream one night. I saw a light (fair) skinned young man wading through a crowd. I could tell that he was very popular amongst them. As I kept watching him, I suddenly woke up. This was a hint of the gender of my third child.

A couple of months later, Chukwuemeka Fredrick arrived after a few hours of labour pains, unlike his siblings that arrived after prolonged labour. All our children were delivered at Margaret's Hospital Umuahia owned by my uncle, Dr Elekwachi Nwaogbo. Charlie was happy, and at peace knowing I was at my uncle's facility. This reassured him, especially as he was still far away at work, during the births of our children.

Charlie and I often sat and shared the dreams we had about our children. He asked me to come up with their Igbo names, while he gave them their English names. Although we were going through such a tough time, we were so close that we hardly ever made decisions independently of each other, except in emergencies of course.

When Emeka arrived, Charlie fondly called him 'yellow man,' because he was very fair in complexion. After three months of being on maternity leave, I returned to work. This time I asked for a transfer to Owerri and it was granted.

After resuming work, in no time with the added pressure of looking after three children, and a husband away in another city, it began to take its toll. I truly thank God for my parents who were simply golden. Charlie even offered to leave his program and come home to be with me. I however encouraged him to carry on as he was. We had sacrificed so much to come this far, and giving up was never an option. We don't quit, instead we look to God, and forge ahead.

I eventually applied to the same university Charlie was in, for a diploma in hospital administration. The programme was for a year, but it was much better than being apart any longer. This automatically meant that the kids and I would have to relocate to Benin City and we did. It gave us the peace of mind we hoped it would, albeit short lived. While waiting for my admission letter, I became very unwell, lost my appetite, and so much weight. It got so bad that I couldn't keep anything down, not even fluid. This became such a matter of concern that Charlie came home for the weekend and took me back with him to get some treatment. I started feeling better but lacked energy and still had some symptoms. No one knew what exactly was the problem, but they were treating me symptomatically.

I had another dream where a man came to me and told me what medication to buy. When I woke up and shared this with Charlie, he told me it was an anti-acid medication used to neutralise, excess acid in the stomach. I asked him to buy this for me, and after a few days, I was a different person. I was healed. Praise God!!

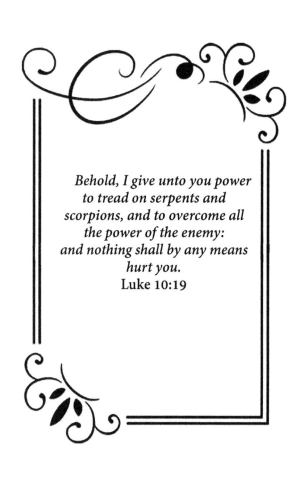

*Behold, I give unto you power
to tread on serpents and
scorpions, and to overcome all
the power of the enemy:
and nothing shall by any means
hurt you.*
Luke 10:19

CHAPTER 7

HIS MERCIES NEVER FAIL

We were both on very basic pay with three children to care for, and we were both studying at the same time. Charles had started taking his fellowship exams, and so far he had passed the Nigerian board exam, but still had the West African examination yet to take.

Around that time, we received an invitation to attend the Full Gospel Business Men's Fellowship meeting and we did. I felt that nudge in my spirit to get serious with my relationship with God, so I stood up when prompted by the preacher, and rededicated my life to the Lord. To my greatest surprise, Charlie also stood up and accepted Jesus. We were overjoyed, and nothing else mattered. The prayer that had been on my lips for so long had finally been answered. Hallelujah!!

On many occasions, God showed himself faithful and provided for us miraculously. One day, I had given the children the last meal that we had in the house. In all honesty we didn't know where our next meal would come from. Charles came back from work that day, opened his car boot and called out to me. When I went to have a look, I saw the boot full of food! Tears of joy rolled down my cheeks as I witnessed that God is indeed so faithful.

Charlie explained that a patient's grateful husband came back to say thank you, after the safe delivery of his wife and child. Everything we needed was in that car. The Lord had provided, and he continued to provide all through our stay in Benin City. We did not lack a single thing!

During one of the trips Charlie had to make to take his exams, I was home alone with the children, and the boys started running very high temperatures. I had no medication to give them, and I remember Ugo's temperature being so high that he had started to twitch, like a child about to convulse. It was around 2am and I didn't know what to do, and there was no one to call at that time of the night. I did the only thing I could do; I knelt down and cried to the Lord, and rebuked the fever at the same time.

I carried on tepid sponging them down to try and break the fever, until they both fell asleep. By the time they awoke the next morning, the fever was gone. They were both fine. Glory to God Almighty who answers when we call on him! Hallelujah!!

During our stay, Charles had to pick up extra work to earn a passive income. On one occasion I accompanied him to an interview. Shortly after the interview ended, I asked him how it went. He explained that the owner of the clinic wanted him to terminate pregnancies as part of his job. He objected saying it was against his Christian faith, but the employer remained adamant. He told him that he wasn't there to play God and if he wanted the job, it was his for the taking. He was however required to terminate pregnancies as a condition of getting the job. Well Charlie firmly refused, adding that he would rather be hungry than soil his hands with innocent blood! Shortly afterwards he found himself a good job that helped us, for the rest of our stay in Benin City.

We went to church one Sunday morning and as it was the custom during offering time, everyone got up from their seat and danced to the front, to put their offering in the bag. I had nothing to put in the offering bag, but I still danced to the front joyfully, placed my hand on my chest, opened up my fisted hand placing that into the offering bag. I gave my heart. I was happy I did.

The last verse of the popular Christmas carol, 'In the bleak Mid-Winter,' comes to mind: w*hat can I give him poor as I am, if I were a shepherd, I would give a lamb: if I were a wiseman, I will do my part: yet what I can I give him, give my heart.* I gave my heart and God honoured that.

Finally I completed my course in Benin and then returned to Owerri and went back to work. The children went back to school and dad gracefully continued to do the school runs for us. He always shared the story of how one day he went to pick them up from school, but when he got there the boys were not there. The school said they thought he'd picked them up already. Like every grandparent would, he panicked. He drove back home to check if some else had dropped them off but they were not there.

After about two good hours of searching for them, he suddenly saw them walking back home exhausted and hungry. Ugochukwu explained that they had been waiting and Emeka thought that since Dede (their grand-dad), was taking too long, they should walk home. Ugochukwu tried to stop Emeka but when he couldn't, he thought it best to join him. Needless to say they didn't try that again.

Charlie passed his West African Fellowship Examination to the glory of God, and got a job with Shell BP. Things began to change for us and although it was a very good job, he soon had to give it up and come back home because of family ties. We'd been apart for too long and our family needed to be together.

In the process of getting back together, I continued to attend the Full Gospel Business Men's fellowship near us. We also became members of a Pentecostal church, called Winners Chapel and things were great. I had an encounter with the Lord one morning. I woke up from sleep and knelt down to pray. The moment I knelt down, I saw a white cloud spiralling in front of me and I passed out. When I woke up, I was mumbling some words I couldn't understand, but I felt so much peace and love around me. Charlie was still in Benin city at this time so when I went to bible study at our Full Gospel chapter, I shared this experience with the people there. The president of the chapter then, Bishop Stafford Nwaogu explained that it had been a visitation from the Lord. The Lord gave me other dreams and visions after that. Some of them were clear and accurate to the last detail. It helped me to pray specifically for people. I totally immersed myself into the Full Gospel Business Men's fellowship (FGBMF for short). I began serving in the area of worship and intercession.

I remember returning from a FGBMF meeting one evening, and I went straight to see my parents. As we were chatting and catching up, a very fierce wind came into the room and started blowing things about. The windows and doors were open so it was easy for the wind to get in and affect things. My spirit however was instantly stirred, and I recognised it wasn't just ordinary wind. I realised that the devil was trying to cause havoc and confusion.

Subsequently the Spirit of God in me took over and I declared loudly, *"Peace be still!"* We were all surprised because the fierce wind ceased instantly and dad joked saying, "You should pass by from Full Gospel meetings anytime," and we laughed about it.

The truth is that as children of God, we need to realise that we have been given power to put the devil in his place at any time.

> *Behold, I give unto you power to tread on serpents and*
> *scorpions, and to overcome all the power of the enemy:*
> *and nothing shall by any means hurt you.*
> **Luke 10:19**

My desire as a new Christian was to serve God and to have my household serve him too, and I really thank God for his faithfulness and grace to do so.

Charlie returned back home and started a new job, as a consultant Obstetrician at General Hospital Owerri. Not long afterwards, he got a letter inviting him to travel to the United kingdom for further training and a Fellowship exam. This was welcome news and a desired next step for his career progression.

As we were preparing for him to travel, he had to let his mother 'Mama Nekede,' know about the new turn of events. He had lost his dad, 'Papa Nekede,' the previous year. He was a jolly fellow, very easy going and kind and is sorely missed even to this day.

Mama Nekede was very happy for Charlie but had mixed feelings. Having recently lost her husband, she knew she would miss Charlie a lot more than she usually would have. She was particularly worried that he would not have access to pounded yam in the UK. She honestly believed that he wouldn't last long in the UK, if there was no access to pounded yam. She did however eventually give her blessing, after being reassured of the ample availability of pounded yam, in what was to be her son's new home.

CHAPTER 8

GOD HAS A PLAN

During one of our prayer sessions before Charlie (Eze) travelled, God gave me a word for him, which he used to confirm his plans for him. This was from *Genesis 12:1-3*

> *Now the LORD had said to Abram: "Get out of your country, From your family, And from your father's house, To a land that I will show you. I will make you a great nation; I will bless you And make your name great; And you shall be a blessing. I will bless those who bless you, And I will curse him who curses you; And in you all the families of the earth shall be blessed.*
> *Genesis 12:1-3*

This was comforting and I held unto it, knowing that God had gone ahead of him. The separation was an emotional one but as God would have it, it didn't last long. Three months later, we joined him.

Our first point of call was a small quiet town called Western Super Mare, where he worked in the Obstetrics and Gynaecology department. He was employed by the Western general hospital as a senior house officer. This was the case although he had been a consultant back home, it was just the way the programme was structured.

We didn't have an easy time settling in, but because Charlie (Eze) had done some ground work, it helped. The children were enrolled in school and we started to worship at the local Church of England, which was just a stone throw from the hospital where we lived.

One day I dressed up in my Sunday best to go to church. When I arrived there, I realised that my outfit was drawing a lot of attention, especially because I was in the choir.

After the service, many people asked me questions about my outfit. As we walked home, even more people stared at this black family in town. They knew Charlie, but seeing the children and I, made it obvious that his family had joined him. We were the only black people in that part of Weston Super-Mare, which made it easy to spot us. People seemed fascinated! We made friends very quickly and were subsequently invited to dinners and we hosted our fair share too!

One time we were invited to a Full Gospel Business Men's fellowship. The speaker asked people to come forward for prayers, and for their families to stand behind them. Charlie stepped forward and I had to stand behind him. Someone walked up to me from behind, and gave me a word from the Lord. They told me that if I continued to serve God as I had done without holding back, that he would bless me greatly. I was pleasantly surprised but very thankful.

On our way back home from the meeting, we talked about the word given and the prayer Charlie received. I held unto the prophecy I received, as encouragement to keep me going. I knew I had never held back in my service to God, and he had never let me down. This time was not going to be different.

It would have been very easy for me to maintain a low key life in the UK, but God had a different plan. Back in

Nigeria, I was a worship leader in our local Full Gospel Chapter, I was also in the prayer group, and an all-round active member of my church. It was not so straight forward here. Since we were in this new environment, I had to find a way to get involved with the activities of the church like I was back home. Although I was in the choir, it wasn't enough.

Shortly after that, I was working at a General hospital, for my Nursing orientation so I could begin practicing as a trained Nurse in line with the UKCC (United Kingdom Central Council for Nursing, Midwifery and Health Visiting). This was an opportunity to meet the requirements. Unfortunately I experienced racism first hand. I was subjected to unfair shift patterns, cold treatment, and I was taken advantage of. The list was endless.

Charlie was in Weston-Super-Mare alone with the Children, and once again life became very tough for us. It was a difficult but necessary stage in our lives, in order to attain the level of career and financial freedom we needed. Thankfully the Lord was with us, and granted us grace and immense favour.

During the time of my orientation I became a woman of few words, saying only what was needed, and straight to the point at all times. I had seen in the scriptures that Jesus only said what he heard his Father say, and I knew that I needed to be like that. This was a key for me to stay out of trouble.

I remember being on duty with one of my good friends, and towards the end of our shift, our patient needed pastoral care and had asked for prayers, so I offered to pray for them. This however made the staff nurse very angry with me, because she said it had to be the Chaplain. Apparently only he was allowed to pray with patients. I received a warning for it, and was assured of disciplinary action if such a thing reoccurred. It was really shocking to me that I could get into trouble, for simply offering to pray for someone.

After the incident, I decided it was best to keep my head down and carry on with my training. Soon enough I noticed that everyone on the ward started watching me, and giving their feedback, including the cleaners and domestic staff.

My patients however loved me and often requested for me to do certain things for them, even when other nurses had been assigned to them. They even wrote references for me, and told me that if I ever had any issues with getting a job when I finished, I was to let them know. I could relate to Joseph in the days of the bible. Not only did I find favour with my patients, but also with the chief Nurse of the hospital. She was also a Christian and took particular interest in me. Sometimes she called me into her office to encourage me. This proved to me that God was watching my back as he always had done. Five months later, I was able to re-join my family who were now in Bangor North Wales.

Before my Nursing and Midwifery Council registration came through, I volunteered on the wards to keep my skills up and to learn the culture. Before long there was an opening on one of the wards, to do bank shifts so I took it. In the meantime I was also learning to drive, so I could help Charlie out with errands and other responsibilities.

Our church in Bangor was a Pentecostal church, and we loved being there as it felt a lot like home. There was a musical production going on at this time called 'The Witness.' It was about the life of Jesus Christ, told in drama and music. It was great and we travelled around the county, presenting it and winning many to Christ through it. The music and drama was mass produced as records, and sold all over the country. At the peak of the tour, I was called and offered bank shifts for two weeks straight, but I turned the shifts down. Although we needed the money, serving God came first and I was very content with that.

After the tour, my PIN number came through which meant I could work as a trained Nurse and start my career in the UK. I chose to start as a nurse so I could learn the culture first, even though I had the options of also working as a midwife or health visitor.

In the same week I had a call notifying me of a vacancy that had recently opened up, and required me to start working within 2-3 days. I was informed that I didn't have to attend an interview, because I was already doing bank shifts for them. As a matter of fact I completed my application on the first day that I started work. It had to be God! He made a way for me yet again.

I became friends with a Christian nurse who attended the same church as I did, and worked on the same ward. She helped me a lot because they spoke welsh freely on the ward, and even handed over patients in welsh which was another problem. Shortly after I complained, I came under the spot light again, but God gave me favour.

Charlie was excelling in his work but needed to get into their rotational scheme for his fellowship examination, so he started applying for jobs to help him to do so. He had limited time to pass the exam before his visa expired. This could have proved to be a major problem, because it was on his visa that we had all joined him. If it expired, then our immigration status would become questionable.

In August 1995 we moved to Walsall in West Midlands where Charlie got a job with Walsall Manor Hospital. It incorporated rotations to Sandwell General Hospital and Birmingham Women's Hospital. Once again the problem was solved. Praise God!

We had to look for a church close to our new home, so I looked through the directory for local churches. I found a Pentecostal church very close to the Manor hospital where we lived. The following Sunday, we decided to check it out. Our plan was for Charlie and I to try a few of the churches around, and then choose one. We wanted a bible believing church, where we would be spiritually well fed.

As we walked in, we were warmly greeted by this very cheerful lady who introduced herself as Velma Henry. She asked us a few questions and linked us up with other nurses and doctors in the church, who lived close to the hospital as well. We felt right at home.

During the service, the senior Pastor John Price announced that it was vision Sunday. He then went ahead and talked about the beliefs and values of the church. It was as if God sent us to the church on that Sunday to see that this is where we were meant to be. Needless to say, we didn't bother looking for any other church. From that day till now we still worship there. It was called the Walsall Evangelistic Centre then, but now it is known as the Church at Junction Ten.

It has been a place of tremendous blessing to say the least. All our children were water baptised there, and we later celebrated our 25th wedding anniversary there also, so the church means a lot to us as a family.

Having found a church for us, I had to wait for the children to settle into their new school, and Charlie into his new job before I could start looking for a job which I did. In October 1996, I started work at Sandwell General hospital. It was a very busy ward and still is, but the team bonding was exceptional, thanks to Rose Butler, the senior Nurse at the time. That's what kept us all going in the midst of working with some difficult people, as well as having to contend with the effects of staff shortages and the challenges of the NHS. (National Health Service).

A good opportunity for career progression came along, and I didn't waste time but took it as soon as I could. I had my visa renewed to an indefinite leave to remain status. A little while later I started a degree, in Health Studies at the University of Wolverhampton. I ended up spending six and half years on that ward. Right at the end, I became one of the discharge planning nurses for the hospital.

For the Lord God is a sun and shield; the Lord will give grace and glory: no good thing will he withhold from those who walk uprightly.
Psalm 84:11

CHAPTER 9

I STILL HAVE JOY

In due course we received news that turned our world upside down. It was December 1999. Charlie came back from work one day and went straight into our bedroom. He called me to come up straight away, which was out of character for him. Normally he joined us where ever we were in the house to check on us, and tell us about his day. Today was different so I hurried up to the room, and he asked me to sit down by his side.

A few weeks before that day, I woke up in the morning and placed my hand on his tummy and realised that one side was harder than the other. When I asked him about it, he said he had no idea what it was, so I insisted he got himself checked out as soon as possible.

When I sat down by his side that day, he told me that the blood results were back, and that it didn't look good. They were suspecting that it was Leukaemia, but we had to wait for the confirmation results, which were due out in a few days' time.

I felt numb and stared into space for what felt like an eternity. My face was immediately flooded with tears flowing freely without restraint. My mind raced with thoughts. *I know it isn't going to be an easy battle but, Almighty God fights all our battles. Surely he didn't bring us all the way from Nigeria for me to be widowed at a young age,* I reasoned with myself. I hugged him tightly and asked him to promise me that he would fight all the way. He promised.

We went down on our knees and cried out from our hearts to God asking Him to take control. We were well aware of our identity in Christ, and knew that God would not give us more than we could handle. God is good. I have a conviction that I've held unto all my life and it goes like this. At whatever stage I find myself, God will only give me what's best for me.

This conviction is based on **Psalm 84:11** and it states:

> *For the Lord God is a sun and shield; the Lord will give grace and glory: no good thing will he withhold from those who walk uprightly.*
> Psalm 84:11

As we knelt there crying and praying, I vowed to fight the enemy with everything I had.

In this new season of our lives, we were careful to keep the information amongst only our family members, church leaders and house group leaders, who joined us in prayer whenever we needed them to. We also informed our employers because we needed as much support as was necessary.

We deliberately stayed away from any negative conversations, and pity parties as the Holy spirit led us. Now in hindsight I see the reason was to guard our hearts from doubts and unbelief, and keep focussed on God. We forgave freely and emptied our hearts of all grudges.

When we felt the time was right, one day we called our children together and Charlie broke the news to them. They were very young and didn't quite understand what

Leukaemia meant, so he took the time to explain it. At the time Uzoma was 15, Ugochukwu was 13 and Emeka was 11.

Charlie called his junior brother Lawrence, who was also a medical doctor at one of the General hospitals near us. Lawrence had joined us in the UK about three years previously. He broke the news to him and it was floods of tears all over again. We also told Obinna my immediate junior brother who lived in London.

In the meantime Charlie and I decided to intensify our family prayers, which had become inconsistent because of work life and shift patterns. We prayed every night and have continued to pray even to this day.

Our children were already believers in Christ at this time, so we took it in turns to pray, sing and recite bible verses. Everyone who came to our house joined in and took this to their houses also. Prayers were going up for us at different units. God took us on a journey of revelations through dreams and visions, some of which I didn't understand then but have witnessed decades later.

A few days after the diagnosis was confirmed, I had another dream. In it I saw a grey haired old man, dressed very casually in a white T-shirt and wrapper round his waist. He was walking leisurely around his compound when I heard a voice say, "the old man's blood matched." I woke up and shared the dream with Charlie. Two days later, we received the news that Lawrence (my brother in-law) who had been tested earlier was a suitable match for the bone marrow transplant!

By this time, Charlie had gone through the initial phase of the treatment to get his blood levels down and prepare his body for the treatment. The stem cells were harvested from my brother-in-law and the date was set. On the appointed date, Charlie had the bone transplant and stayed in hospital for a good number of weeks.

Subsequently he had stopped work and didn't return to work for just over a year.

I was working full time and at the same time taking my degree examination. The children also were at very critical stages in their school work. Carol (Uzoma) was taking her GCSE and the boys were taking exams also. Ugo especially was very quiet and wouldn't open up at all, while Emeka was his usual self barely understanding what was going on. I was on the road a lot, driving from one place to place. Life was so difficult.

We received words of prophecy from people who were praying for us. One of them came through a very good friend of ours. It was based on a word from Isaiah 37 about Hezekiah. It was about how the man of God had given him a word to set his life in order, because he was going to die. In response Hezekiah set his face against the wall and cried unto the Lord and God answered him and gave him fifteen more years.

Another word from **Psalm 112:6-8** which states:

> *Surely he will never be shaken; The righteous will be in everlasting remembrance. He will not be afraid of evil tidings; His heart is steadfast, trusting in the LORD. His heart is established; He will not be afraid, Until he sees his desire upon his enemies.*
>
> Psalm 112:6-8

Charlie held this to heart as we prayed day and night, and we sensed the presence and peace of God. Physically the treatment took its toll on him. He lost weight and hair, he suffered nausea, diarrhea and a very low immunity.

He read his bible on the ward and witnessed to the nurses and doctors, and became known as the praying patient. As time went on, the nurses brought prayer requests, asking him to pray for other patients on the ward. Spiritually he was doing really well.

I remember travelling straight from his bed side to the university to take some of my exams. It was the same for our daughter Carol. She was very tearful and anxious and the whole thing had affected her badly.

I was coming back from the hospital one day and the Lord gave me a word from: *2 Corinthians 4:7-10*

> *But we have this treasure in earthen vessels, that the excellence of the power may be of God and not of us. We are hard-pressed on every side, yet not crushed; we are perplexed, but not in despair; persecuted, but not forsaken; struck down, but not destroyed, always carrying about in the body the dying of the Lord Jesus, that the life of Jesus also may be manifested in our body.*
>
> 2 Corinthians 4:7-10

How comforting I found this!

I was still going to work and attending church and house group meetings in the midst of everything. There was a lot of suffering and pain, but we had joy and an unexplainable inner strength. We put God at the centre of everything.

Before this time, we were strong committed Christians alright, but our lives had been more about our careers, work, family and so on. Suddenly this phase made us see life from a completely different perspective. When the diagnosis was confirmed, I promised God in prayer that if he healed my husband, I would serve him for the rest of my days, and tell people about him and not be silent. Some of the things I know now, I didn't know then. I had made a Covenant with the Lord without even knowing it. I have come to know and understand that our God is a covenant keeping God. He never fails!

Before long, God proved himself faithful. One of the testimonies of our journey was that we depended on the Lord for sustenance, direction and everything else, and he came through for us. One of the songs that Charlie loved to sing was, 'I still have joy,' by Ron Kennoly and 'I don't mind waiting,' by Juanita Bynum. We sang these songs to keep us joyful and Praise conscious at all times. We were not going to let the enemy steal our joy.

Our family, friends and church family continually prayed for us. They often visited us at home, or in the hospital to encourage us, pray or support us in other ways. Praise God eventually Charlie was discharged. He still had to go for check-ups regularly. During one of those visits, he received news that was music to his ears. All the cancer cells in his blood had gone. The Lord had set him free!

The hospital appointments became less frequent but as time went on, he developed a condition they called graft versus host disease. The donated bone marrow and the recipient's bone marrow were fighting each other. Apparently this was normal and expected to some extent. It was not a problem as long as it did not become severe. If it did, it could result in other organs of the body getting damaged.

One of the reactions Charlie experienced were blisters on his legs. I had to dress them for him at home and administer other types of home treatment. The leg dressing was very humbling for him, but he handled it very well, with positive words and affirmations. He would always exclaim that, "Jesus is Lord," every now and again.

Carol was very supportive as she helped me and sat with him while she read and prepared for her GCSE exams. Ugo just couldn't handle it emotionally, and he always sat around the house in deep thought. Emeka was too young to even understand the details of what was going on, but somehow we managed as God was on our side.

PART 3

CHAPTER 10

CAST YOUR EYES ON JESUS

At this point in time, I must confess that we need to be careful who we allow to come into our homes. People are not always who they make themselves out to be. Unfortunately we experienced this first hand. Charlie and I loved people and we always had visitors in our home. We considered it a blessing to be able to bless others in that way.

We decided to help a distant relative by facilitating her visa, standing in for her as next of kin. We provided shelter and had her welfare at heart for a long period of time. Little did we know that we had given our pearls to swine! Before long it was thrown back in our faces. Once she got what she wanted, everything about her changed. Whatever she heard us say or saw us do, became public knowledge, thanks to her loose tongue, constantly making us objects of ridicule and hot topics for gossip.

We dined with the enemy without realising it. She tried to cause contention between Charlie and I and even our children. Thankfully the revealer of mysteries intervened, and things came to light. It all climaxed during one of Charlie's hospital admissions.

On three separate occasions Charlie had to be readmitted to hospital, because of an unexplained high temperature. They feared his kidneys could be affected if things didn't settle. We became concerned and as I was praying, the Lord gave me a word saying, "It's time to separate Abraham and Lot."

One day I was at home doing my chores so that I could get back to the hospital, to see Charlie and drop off some food. I also had to run a few errands and attend my lectures. Eventually I managed to finish my chores and subsequently left the house. It was a one-way trip with many stops which took quite some time. Our children were in school and our guest was at home when I left. She didn't want to help as apparently she had other plans.

When our children returned home from school, they were locked out of the house without food or drink for hours. Our guest had locked the house and left to go out somewhere. When I called the landline to check up on them, there was no response and we became worried. At about 7pm, since I was still unable to get an answer on the phone, I had no choice but to rush back from the hospital, to see what was going on at home.

To my shock and horror, I arrived to find the children standing outside and almost hypothermic which broke my heart. I quickly took them inside, warmed them up, fed and observed them, until they were able to talk a bit.

When I called Charlie to let him know what had happened, he was very angry. He explained that our guest turned up at the hospital unannounced, and she had the key to the house. I rushed back to the hospital and when I got there, Charlie informed me that he had asked our guest to look for alternative accommodation, and leave our house within two weeks.

I knew that decision was of God because I hadn't even discussed with him about the word I had received earlier on that day. With everything going on with his health, I didn't want him to be upset or stressed out at all.

It was a dark winter night and tipping down with rain. Driving home from the hospital was very awkward, because I still had to go back home with our guest. You could have cut the atmosphere with a knife. It was however through God's saving grace that we escaped what could have been a bad car accident that night. All through the journey back, our guest did not utter a word.

What transpired later was that our guest had planned to leave the house without letting us know. As it happened we had popped out to get something and just as we arrived back home, a taxi had pulled up at the house, to take her to her new place. If we hadn't seen her outside, she would have left without our knowledge. Right there and then, we blessed her and told her that we forgave her, and had nothing against her.

About fifteen minutes after she left, we literally saw dark clouds shift away from our home. We became joyful, and sang and rejoiced. Charlie said it was time for celebration and he went out and got some KFC for everyone. The joy was very palpable, and that was the last time he was readmitted into hospital for this episode of illness. We have learned to bless people no matter what, because vengeance is not ours but the Lord's. We carried on being a blessing, even after our guest moved out of our home.

During this time, Charlie didn't go to work for over a year. We were happy and we managed very well. We lacked nothing really, because we know that God is faithful and never forsakes his own. Like the apostle Paul, we had learned over the years, to be abased and how to abound.

Charlie had a friend whom we had welcomed into to our home for a few days, when he first came into the country. Soon afterwards he moved into his own place ready to start his new job. When he heard what had happened to Charlie, he made a commitment to give a monetary gift to my husband, for as long as he was off work. He fulfilled this pledge to the very end, and at one point Charlie had to beg him to stop. "The Lord Bless and replenish Dr O! You and yours will always be remembered by us forever."

God supernaturally guided us through this rough patch, and brought us through to a rich fulfilment. *Isaiah 43 verse 2* was one of Charlie's favourite scriptures at the time and it states:

> *When you pass through the waters, I will be with you;*
> *And through the rivers, they shall not overflow you.*
> *When you walk through the fire, you shall not be*
> *burned, Nor shall the flame scorch you.*
> Isaiah 43:2

He literally lived this scripture as God was truly with him in everything. The Lord brought him through all the challenges, and we always had a testimony on our lips. The Lord showed me through dreams when Charlie was to be discharged. I would in turn go prepared and whenever I got there, it was exactly the way the Lord had showed it to me.

In one of the dreams, I was standing in front of the first floor balcony of a building, and I saw a man dressed in a long white robe with outstretched arms. There was so much light coming from his chest area, revealing his heart and I felt the love of God like never before. I knew this was the Lord's way of reassuring us, that he was indeed with us, and that my friend, was very reassuring. It was really all that mattered to us.

On another occasion I had a dream where I was sitting alone at a white round table, as if waiting for someone to dine with. It was set in an open field and there were other dinners there too, but my table was dressed in a white over flowing cloth. There appeared in front of me a rainbow, and I knew immediately that the covenant keeping God was on my side, and I didn't need to be afraid of anything.

I also had dreams where I knew everyone would be at home, and I would hear Charlie's voice but not see him, but I would have that assurance that he is around me somewhere.

The dreams carried on but they were not always good dreams. The enemy tried to creep in to abort our testimony, but we resisted him out-rightly. One such instance was when I was in a room and someone pushed in two coffins, a big one and a small one. I immediately got up, opened the door and kicked out both coffins, and then I woke up in a pool of sweat. I prayed and cancelled it straight away, because the scripture tells us in *Mathew 18:18,*

> *Verily I say unto you, whatsoever ye bind on earth*
> *shall be bound in heaven: and whatsoever ye*
> *loose on earth shall be loosed in heaven.*
> **Mathew 18:18**

I often shared my dreams with Charlie and we always prayed a prayer of agreement, and cancelled those dreams that we didn't want. Our evening prayers were quite special and became our time of bonding. In the mornings, we also had our separate quiet times so we could each hear God for ourselves. It was at this time that I developed a disciplined prayer life, of rising early to pray before my family woke up. I received guidance from the Holy spirit for each day, and for weeks and sometimes months ahead.

On one occasion, a friend of Charlie's who lived in Wales had received a message from the Lord and called him. He didn't know Charlie wasn't feeling quite well, but he travelled all the way from wales to come and pray for him. He explained to Charlie how God had put a burden on his heart to leave everything he was doing, to visit him that night! During the prayers, the presence of God filled the whole house and was very tangible. Charlie fell under the anointing of the Holy spirit and muttered words that no one in the room knew as he was filled with the spirit of God. When he recollected himself, he was a new man, Praise God!! Thank you, Dr Sam for being obedient to the spirit of God.

Shortly afterwards, another friend of Charlie's invited him for a business meeting in a hotel. I advised him not to go, because it didn't sit well with my spirit. He hadn't even gone back to work yet, and was still building himself up. He didn't listen to me however, and went for the meeting anyway.

When he got back home he complained that the venue was full of smokers, and he wasn't comfortable so he had to leave. That exposure affected him negatively, to the point that he began to feel unwell. Before long we had to go to the hospital because he started getting chest pains. He had to be kept in for an angiogram, but afterwards he was told that he had no business on the cardiac ward, and was subsequently discharged.

A few weeks later he was offered a locum job, which I advised him to turn down until his health improved. He decided however to take the job to help him get back to normal. A few days later however we knew something was wrong. This time things turned serious and he had to be admitted into hospital. He had to undergo a Bronchoscopy, which showed that he had developed Pneumonia. Before he went in for the procedure, he apologised to me for going for that locum job. We prayed together and committed everything to God. After the investigation, his breathing changed and they feared the worse.

24 A man that hath friends must
shew himself friendly:
and there is a friend that sticketh
closer than a brother.
Proverbs 18:24

CHAPTER 11
A FRIEND IN TIME OF NEED

When you are called into a side room in the hospital with the consultant and some nurses, then you know it is not going to be good news. I pulled myself together and listened to all they had to say. They reminded me of all the complications that could happen, and I remember her uttering the phrase, "This is it!"

At that moment the Spirit of God welled up on the inside of me, and I was bold enough to respond without fear. I thanked her and replied, "I understand you have spoken to me, based on the results of the investigations carried out and I respect that. However I have a God who has promised never to leave us or forsake (abandon) us. My God whom I serve, is strong and mighty, and will see my husband through. He will make a full recovery!" I declared boldly.

I thanked them and left the room. As I walked out I could see the look of pity on their faces, but I paid them no mind. I simply went straight to Charlie's bed side and sat down. I called him but he didn't answer, because he was completely zonked out from the medication they gave him, during the procedure. I called him again, a little louder and shook him this time. I reminded him that he used to tell me that we would grow old together. "If you know you love me, then you need to hang in there for me, and not give up," I reminded him.

When I said that, he opened his eyes and looked at me

as if I was going mad, and went back into a deep sleep.

I held myself together until I got to the car park, and then I let it all out. I cried and screamed, not caring where I was or who was watching me. I started shaking all over and wondered how I was going to get home to see my children, before I was due to come back to the hospital.

Right at that time, the Lord laid it on my friend's heart to call me at that time. I was sobbing when her call came through and could hardly talk. She prayed for me and I honestly cannot remember anything she said. All I knew was that after that prayer, I felt as though a bucket of cold water had been poured on my head.

"Thank you Dr Moe!" I managed to say. Suddenly I was calm enough to drive, so I picked up my car keys and drove home.

I called the children together and we prayed. Once I fed them, I headed back to the hospital that night. I knew the enemy was out to steal, kill and destroy, so I began to pray in the spirit. After a while, Charlie woke up but his saturation was very low, so they gave him intravenous medications and nebulisers at about 3am.

When he felt able, he sat up and shared a dream he'd had. He was in the middle of the sea in a boat, with men dressed in white loin cloths, topless, and clean shaven. He was fighting them because he didn't want to go on that journey and then he woke up. I thanked God that I was there, so we could pray together. We cancelled the dream and declared God's healing over him. When the hospital staff came round again, his parameters had improved and he asked for a drink.

Jesus snatched him out of the hands of the evil one. When the medics came round in the morning during ward round, they could not believe he was the same patient they had seen the night before. They were amazed and agreed that something supernatural had taken place.

A few days later, my husband was discharged and allowed to go home. The nurses and doctors started to ask him to pray for other patients who were poorly, because he was always seen reading his bible, and talking to them about his Christian faith.

God also surrounded us with people of strong faith, who stood by us, prayed for us and with us. Charlie spent so much time in the word, and I knew he had a gift for teaching, because he always gave in-depth views of the word of God that most people wouldn't have even thought of.

His health got better and better each day, and eventually he was fully recovered. During this time after due consideration, he decided it was time for a career change, so this was the start of his career as a General Practitioner (GP). He loved his work as a GP although it had its own challenges, but God was faithful and his love for God came across very strongly. This was evident and his patients began to request to see him specifically, when they attended the surgery. Some of them knew he was a Christian and prayed for him and he prayed for them also.

The senior pastor of our church Pastor John Price asked if we could (as a couple), head up the international group in our Church. We did not hesitate to say yes, because we had made a promise to the Lord to serve him if Charlie was healed. We saw it as an opening and accepted the challenge.

It became a very dynamic group of about 63 people at the time from 13 different countries. We had to grow in the role and we saw many people retained in our church, as other people moved from one church to another, either due to the nature of their jobs or because they needed a church that felt like home to them.

It was a lot of fun being part of the Church at Junction Ten. During our time of leadership of this group, the international day celebration became a church event to look forward to every year. We led this group for 9 years, before we moved on to other things that we felt God was calling us into.

Charlie was very involved in the house group and Saturday early morning prayers. I was in the intercessory group and attended the Saturday morning prayer meetings too. These were valued times with God, and every opportunity we had to serve we took, because we knew what God had brought us through. We served with joy and gratitude to God, and not out of obligation. Every opportunity Charlie had to share his testimony was a bonus for him. I even had a dream about him standing on a podium and preaching, with his bible in his hand. I shared this with him at the time.

Many people were blessed, and encouraged by his testimony and he made it a point of duty, to support others who went through similar problems, either in prayer or financially. I remember when I felt strongly called to evangelise in the streets. This also came to me in a dream.

CHAPTER 12

HEEDING THE CALL OF GOD

I was walking down this street in the dream and chatting with people when a man came up to me and said, "Do it as they did in *Acts 10:30-47.*"

When I woke up, I read this portion of scripture which I would encourage you to read in your own time. For now I will paraphrase it this way:

There was a man called Cornelius, a centurion and a devout man who feared God and gave much alms to people. He was a praying man, and an angel of God appeared to him in a vision and told him his prayers were answered, and that his giving had come up to God as a memorial.

The angel asked him to send men to Joppa and ask for Simon Peter who would tell him what he needed to do. So, he chose three men and explained to them what the Lord had told him in that vision, and sent them to Joppa the following day.

Now Peter went to the house top to pray and while he was there, he became very hungry and fell into a trance and he saw the heaven open a certain vessel descending unto him with all manner of four footed beasts of the earth, wild beasts, and creeping things and fowls of the air and a voice from heaven came to him saying, "Rise, Peter; kill and eat."

But Peter said "not so Lord, for I have never eaten anything that is common or unclean." And the voice came again to him saying, "what God has cleansed; that you must not call common."

This happened three times and the vessel was received up and while he was pondering and doubted in himself what this vision meant, unknown to him, the men Cornelius sent arrived at his gate asking for him and as he thought of the vision, the Holy Spirit of God told him there were three men asking after him and told Peter to go with them and not doubt for the Lord had sent them. Peter lodged the men for the night and the next day, they set off to Caesarea.

Now Cornelius had gathered his household and friends to come and hear the word of God through Peter. Peter began by saying how unlawful it was for a Jew to keep company or come unto one of another nation, but God had showed him not to call any man common or unclean.

Now Cornelius shared with Peter his own encounter with God, that resulted in him sending three of his men to Joppa, to look for him and in verse 33, Cornelius said this,

"Now are we all here present before God, to hear all things that are commanded thee of God."

Peter admitted that God is no respecter of persons but in every nation, he that fears God and is righteous, is accepted. God does not cast off anyone who comes to him, because he is a loving Father, and he is Lord of all. Now Peter preached to them about how Jesus Christ of Nazareth went about doing good, healing all that were oppressed of the devil, and how Jesus went to the Jews.

He also told them how Jesus went to Jerusalem where he was killed, hung on a tree. He himself and others had been witnesses of this. God raised Him up on the third day, he appeared to them after the resurrection, and commanded them to be witnesses. He also shared that whosoever believes in the name of Jesus, shall receive remission of their sins. And while he was speaking, the Holy Spirit fell on all of them that heard the word of God, and they spoke in other tongues, including the Gentiles in their midst, and they were also water baptised.

After reading this Bible scripture, I was so amazed by the way God orchestrates things, putting people together for the furtherance of the gospel. Thinking about it, both Cornelius and Peter were praying when the Lord told them what to do. God is always very specific with such things, and always reveals his divine plan to those who are seeking him, those who are available, and those who are willing.

Both men didn't know each other before, but when they eventually met, there was no confusion. God had already revealed it to them separately, and prepared them about what was about to come.

There are many places in scripture, where God demonstrated that he is the master planner of our lives, and he makes things work together for the good of the gospel and for our good also.

Another such place is found in *Acts 9: 1-15*, where Paul formerly named Saul set out to kill Christians on his way to Damascus. On this journey, he encountered the Lord and suddenly a bright light from heaven shone around him, and he fell to the ground, and heard a voice call him.

"Saul, Saul, why are you persecuting Me? And he said, "Who are you, Lord?" Then the Lord said, "I am Jesus, whom you are persecuting. It is hard for you to kick against the goads." So he, trembling and astonished, said, "Lord, what do You want me to do? Then the Lord said to him, "Arise and go into the city, and you will be told what you must do."

The men who went with him heard the voice, but saw no one and it left them speechless. When Saul arose from the ground, he was blind and had to be led by his companions into Damascus. He was there blind and couldn't eat or drink.

At the same time there was a certain disciple named Ananias, who lived in Damascus. The Lord appeared to him in a vision:

"So the Lord said to him, "Arise and go to the street called Straight, and inquire at the house of Judas for one called Saul of Tarsus, for behold, he is praying. And in a vision he has seen a man named Ananias coming in and putting his hand on him, so that he might receive his sight."

Now Ananias in response, tried to remind God of the many evil deeds Saul had done to the believers at Jerusalem, and how he had authority to bind all that called on the name of Jesus. However this is what the Lord said to Ananias, *"Go, for he is a chosen vessel of Mine to bear My name before Gentiles, kings, and the children of Israel."*

Ananias went to the address the Lord gave him and found Saul there. Brother Saul narrated to him his encounter on the way to Damascus. Ananias explained to him that Jesus had sent him, to come and pray for him, that he might receive his sight and be filled with the Holy Ghost. And when Ananias laid hands on him, scales fell from his eyes and he received his sight immediately, and he arose and was baptised.

When he had eaten and refreshed himself, he stayed some days with the disciples in Damascus, and then he went straight from there to the synagogues and began to preach the gospel straight away.

God is a good God and he knows all about us, including where we live, and what our names are. He has our future all mapped out, and he has plans for us. As you can see from the above, it doesn't matter whether we are Jews or Gentiles, white or black, male or female, God has plans for us all.

In *1 Peter 2:5* it states:

You believers, like living stones, are being built up into a spiritual house for a holy and dedicated priesthood, to offer spiritual sacrifices that are acceptable and pleasing to God through Jesus Christ.
1 Peter 2:5

We are all special before God and he has plans for us. Every precious stone has its place in this spiritual house, that is being built up. I certainly wouldn't want my place to be vacant. Now I've referenced all those scriptures, to mention that after reading *Acts 10*, I pondered it in my heart and meditated on it for a long time and not knowing how things were going to pan out. In myself however, I was willing and ready to serve.

I shared this with my husband because we always did things together and supported each other. He was happy for me, and ready to support me knowing that this might mean, opening up our home to other people. I had contacted my neighbours and some friends and someone to come and preach in my house. While this was going on, I attended a prophetic ministry conference at the Amblecote Christian centre in Dudley, West midlands. I went to listen to Martin Scott teach on the gift of prophecy. We were asked to stand in two rows, to close our eyes, to pray for the person in front of us, and hear what God was saying to us about them.

The person who stood behind me happened to be one of the people doing the training. He said he saw a pair of trainers when he was praying for me, and went on to say that he saw me going to prayer walk areas, maybe locally, maybe from town to town.

He said he sensed it very strong and again, I kept that in mind.

Afterwards I began to have dreams and visions where I was given a pair of shoes, or where I would have a shoe in front of me. I continued praying and fasted specifically concerning this for clarity. It was at this point that one of my church pastors was introducing the missional communities. This involved members with specific gifting or calling in particular areas, being given a free rein to develop their gifts. To apply the principles of Missional community, your ministry had to have a missional statement, a purpose and a missional or outreach aspect to it. There had to be time for fellowship in the church, building up each other with the word of God, and of course there was also the reaching out (The up, the in and the out).

As I sat and listened to this presentation, my heart started warming up and I could feel heat flow through my body. I knew immediately that this was the time to step out. After the meeting therefore, I indicated my interest straight away. I felt I didn't need to confer with flesh and blood, because I had put parts of the jig saw together, and I knew it was time. What I didn't know was how to start, or who would be involved. I had no clue of the details. All I knew was that I made a promise to serve, and I was going to keep that promise.

As you know, the enemy won't keep quiet and watch you serve God, without trying to distract or interrupt God's plans. However it's also our duty to stop him. We know that we have the authority to trample on snakes and scorpions, and to overcome all the powers of the enemy, and nothing shall by any means hurt us. *(Luke 10:19)*.

Not long afterwards I was called for a routine mammogram, and when the results came back, I was invited for further investigations.

I went for two separate biopsies and after the second one, they referred me to the Oncology Nurse specialist, and assigned me to a consultant because the results were inconclusive and could be cancerous. I had peace but I could tell Charlie was very anxious, because he kept following me around, and watching my every expression and movement. I did understand especially after all we had already been through. We wouldn't have wished any of it even on our worst enemy. All I was concerned about was to fulfil what God had laid on my heart to do.

In my own time, I fasted and prayed and reminded God that I hadn't prayer walked yet, and still wanted to fulfil my purpose. I was ready for whatever the outcome might be, as long as I fulfilled what I knew God was calling me to do.

One day after that as a pastor friend of mine was praying for me, I felt a surge of heat run through my body but I kept it to myself. The next Sunday service, after communion, I felt the heat surge flow again and I knew God had done something for me.

The following week, I got a call from the hospital to say that they were not going to do anything further about the lumps. When I asked why, the response I got was, "why fix what's not broken? You've carried it along all this time and didn't even know that it was there, so don't worry about it. We would however like you to have another mammogram. This all happened in 2010, and there's been no mention of it since, even though I have had about three more scans over the last ten years. God healed me of whatever it was they saw there, because he has work for me to do!

Things were building up and I knew that God was in all of it. Although I didn't even know the next step to take, I trusted God all the way. I remember one of the leaders from my church coming to my house to see me, as I was recuperating from a Thyroidectomy operation. We spent time catching up and praying about this new ministry, and she asked what the name of the ministry would be. I told her I didn't know, but as she prayed for me that day, the Lord dropped the word "Father's Heart" into my spirit.

I kept it to myself as I prayed about it and within one week, this name was confirmed three times on three different occasions. I hope I will have the opportunity to write about 'Father's Heart ministry,' and how far God has brought us. It has been an exciting journey so far and God has been faithful. Ten years on, Father's Heart Ministry of the Church at Junction Ten, is still out there in Bescott market and beyond, being a witness to the glory of God. There has never been a more important time in my life to share the gospel of Jesus Christ than now.

We have been led by the Holy Spirit every step of the way. I certainly didn't know what I was doing and neither did anybody else in the team. Everything was born, and directed in the place of prayer, and God brought alongside us people with experience in different areas of ministry. Therefore we have been very blessed and so has the market.

Looking back now I know the Holy Spirit was teaching us, mentoring and discipling us and showing us how to disciple others. This was important as there was no formal training on evangelism, until years later when some of us had the opportunity to attend some conferences. The Holy Spirit remains our teacher and mentor.

We have seen so many wonderful things happen in the market, and it goes to prove that God can use anybody. HE is not looking for people who are experienced but for those who are willing, available and teachable. To God alone be all the glory for what HE continues to do because we know that greater things are yet to come.

He often felt bad that we were going through so much, and he often said, "I'm so sorry that you have had to go through all this."

CHAPTER 13

THE MAN I CALL CHARLIE

Years later Charlie had other health challenges like Pneumonia and Kidney failure, but in all of this God remained very faithful. Nothing was going to stop Charlie from being himself, serving God and going to work. He never lost his sense of humour. He had pet names for most people around him, and he was full of words of encouragement for everyone.

We saw God's healing hand again and again. He had viral pneumonia on two occasions without even being treated in hospital. It was only confirmation received from tests, that highlighted that he was recovering from the condition.

On this particular day I remember him waking up feeling unwell. We talked about things and agreed it was time to go to hospital to be checked out. I packed up a little bag in case they decided to keep him in, and we prayed and believed God for healing. I started to get ready to accompany him and he suddenly called me and told me to unpack the bag. "I'm well now and there's no need to go to hospital after all," he concluded. Truly he seemed to be okay.

When he went for a routine appointment the following week, he mentioned it to the doctor who decided to run some tests to make sure he was alright. His lungs showed he'd had pneumonia but there were no more symptoms of it, and they even wanted to know where he was treated.

This wasn't a one-off testimony though; because it happened a few times and we are so grateful to God for His faithfulness.

Since he was a doctor himself, his GP and colleagues always made sure he had the best of care. In 2010 it was recommended for him to start dialysis treatment, because of the progressive deterioration of his kidney function. It was difficult to come to terms with this, especially as we had believed God for divine healing. However we felt the best thing to do was to carry on with the treatment option, until they found a match for a kidney transplant.

As he went through dialysis treatment, it was a down time for us but Charlie took it well. He attended the dialysis centre three time a week for treatment, and his sessions were usually in the evenings. He didn't stop work, but carried on as he wanted to and could. He never moaned or showed any sign of frustration. His response whenever asked about his wellbeing was always the same, "Jesus Is Lord!" That was his philosophy in life and a catch phrase for him. He was always with his bible during dialysis sessions, or listening to worship music. He made friends wherever we went and needless to say, God gave him favour.

Later on they gave him the option for home dialysis which we took. It was better because we could do this in our home, and still carry on with life without missing out on anything. We did this for four years and there were no complications whatsoever. It was like having two jobs, because we would come back from work and then start the dialysis session. This would last for about three or four hours on the day of treatment, three times a week. We had our routine and God was with us.

We always prayed before and after dialysis, and during the session he would tune into UCB radio and listen to Derek Prince, Gerrard Cooper, Charles Stanley and Bob Gass. They were his favourite speakers teaching on different topics. Sometimes he watched football matches, played solitaire and also had his evening meal. It was also time for us to catch up and plan things as well. He was my confidant, my greatest critic, a great encourager and I learnt so much from him.

He often felt bad that we were going through so much, and he often said, "I'm so sorry that you have had to go through all this."

"I would rather be with you than anywhere else," I reassured him. He didn't ask for any of this. It was just one of the challenges of life. We were however happy together, and that's all that mattered.

We had a very active social life, as our weekends were usually busy with visits and travels. When we were not out visiting, we would usually be hosting people, and watching one sporting event or the other. He loved sports especially Tennis, and football. Table tennis was his favourite sport, and he had even won awards for table tennis when he was at university. He took the boys especially to play and sometimes they played lawn tennis. That was a time of great bonding for them. They all enjoyed and loved being together although they didn't quite make it to Wimbledon! Uzoma sometimes played with them and at other times just sat and watched.

Charlie also loved bike riding although he wasn't very good at it. However when it came to DIY he was the king of it. He loved dismantling things and putting them back together again. Reading was another passion of his, especially voluminous books. Some of his favourite authors were Jeffrey Archer, Sidney Sheldon, William Shakespeare, and Confucius (Confucius Says) especially in his younger days.

As he got older, it was more Christian books and lots of his leisure time was invested in music. He loved listening to music and enjoyed playing the Key board even though he wasn't an expert. He played with Ugo a lot especially during our family prayer time.

He enjoyed his food but rarely ate outside except on family outings, or certain occasions purely because he was very selective. He had his favourites foods, and although I would cook and keep, he would always wait for me to come back from where ever I had been to, before he would eat. That's because he loved it when we ate together.

After the Lord healed him from Leukaemia, we saw three of our children complete and excel in their secondary education, and universities and the secure good jobs. It was around this time that the Lord gave me a dream about a beautiful sunset and when I woke up, I was quite worried by it, so prayed about it and kept it in mind.

In 2009 we celebrated our 25th wedding anniversary, and that brought our family and friends together, joining us in celebration of God's faithfulness. How can we not thank God for all the things he had done and continues to do for us? During Charlie's speech I remember he used one of his favourite bible scriptures, *"he who finds a good wife, finds a good thing."* He then thanked me for being a good wife and soulmate to him.

My husband was unique, a rare gem, full of wisdom and fearless. What other people whispered, he would feel comfortable announcing to everyone, especially when it had to do with justice. He was a voice for so many and that earned him a lot of admiration. I saw him resolve so many marital disputes that would have resulted in separation or even divorce. He hated injustice to the core, and would do anything to defend those at the receiving end, who couldn't fight for themselves. Little wonder it hit him hard when he found himself at the receiving end.

He hadn't been working long as a GP, when he received a call from the Human Resource's department, asking him to come and complete his pensions form. He collected the form, filled it in and submitted it to them. A few months later he was called in for a meeting. At the meeting he was accused of fraud! Before he knew what was happening, the case was reported to the General Medical council! If he was found guilty, it could result in him being struck off the register, and unable to practise in the United Kingdom! *Oh Boy!* We thought.

This news was most disturbing to him and took a lot out of him. He was a man of integrity who feared God. He was a very hard working and honest man who was content with what he had. Therefore to be accused of trying to defraud anyone, let alone an establishment, was too much to bear but like everything else, we took it to God in prayer.

Building up to his court hearing, Charlie had to get a lawyer to defend him. The organisation had to write to the twenty three GP practices, where Charlie had worked as a locum GP at some point or another. This was necessary to collect evidence. However not a single one of them had anything bad to report or to hand in. That in itself was a glowing testimony of the integrity of the man I married!

It was a panel of 10 jury members and of course the legal teams on both sides. We prayed like never before. As for me, I witnessed spiritual battle first hand, because you could sense that the allegations were falsified and the story fabricated. Thankfully it wasn't long before that came across very strongly. When the chief witness was called to the stand, he was visibly shaking and sweating profusely. This seemed to get worse when he was being interrogated, because his story didn't add up at all. His testimony was neither cogent nor coherent and everyone present at the hearing observed this.

Needless to say, that when this witness was called back a few days later, he refused to come. He said he had nothing against my husband, and didn't know why he was asked to testify against an innocent man!

After months of gathering evidence, and preparing for the hearing and another week in court, Charlie was cleared from the allegation, because they couldn't find any fault against him. When the jury declared their verdict of not guilty, Charlie began to cry. I couldn't hold back my tears either. My heart was broken that such things could be allowed to happen to an innocent man.

God fought this battle and gave Charlie victory and he carried on with his GP career. He kept a safe distance from this organisation that reported him to General Medical Council. He wanted nothing to do with them and maintained minimal links after that incident. I believed strongly that he was set up. The evidence was there for all to see. He didn't initiate the signing of the forms. He was called to complete the forms, only for the very same people to turn round and take him to court.

The God of justice fought for us and gave us victory. Two of his friends who knew about this were exceptionally supportive. My prayer is that God will remember them and bless them in a spectacular way. These are friends that we often shared our Christmas celebrations with. It can be a lonely time for many, so we took it in turns to host and pray together, especially for the coming year. This, did bring us together and make our friendships stronger. We had many other close friends also, but it was difficult to bring everyone together. There were other little clusters in our circle of friends similar to this, at this time of year in the United kingdom.

Trust in the L<small>ORD</small> *with all your heart, And lean not on your own understanding; In all your ways acknowledge Him,*
And He shall direct your paths.

Proverbs 3:5-6

CHAPTER 14

SAVED BY GRACE

In 2012 our first son Ugochukwu Anthony got married to Cynthia. It was a very joyous occasion because we even had our siblings attend and it was a very beautiful celebration.

Emmanuella Ugochinyerem arrived later the same year and two years later Amarachi Mary followed. I remember Charlie calling me grandma and we teased each other with our new identity of 'grandma and grandpa.' Charlie loved our grandchildren a lot and always played with them and cuddled them.

I remember having very severe back pain after Ugo and Cynthia's wedding. It was so unbearable that I couldn't stand up for too long without grabbing a seat for a little respite. My mother was still around after the wedding and she became concerned as well. I was on regular paracetamol but it didn't really touch the pain. Co-codamol was therefore always on my shopping list, whether the GP prescribed it or not, because it was only a reduced dose allowed over the counter.

I knew not to take both medications at the same time as co-codamol contains paracetamol. Charlie persuaded me to go to the GP for further investigations, because we found out that the right side of my back was swollen and painful. After an X-ray and consultation with the GP, he told me that I had arthritis in my back and spine. This wasn't good news because he even went on to say that if the condition becomes progressive, that mobility might become a problem. That concerned me greatly because I couldn't imagine myself in a wheel chair being pushed by anyone! *Who would have the job of pushing me around?* I wondered.

My brother Osondu invited us to 'The Christ Embassy Night of bliss programme,' in London and Charlie and I went along. I had faith and was eager for Charlie to be healed, and didn't actually think of myself. We sat next this young man who was very intrusive. During the praise and worship session, he spread his hands so much that he kept covering our faces! He acted as if he was the only person in the whole auditorium. He was really getting on people's nerves and Charlie wasn't happy. I advised and encouraged him to take no notice and try to focus, so that he wouldn't be distracted. The arena was packed and we couldn't change our seats.

The worship session was beautiful and so was the preaching and testimonies. I didn't go out to be prayed for, but instead sat down and prayed along with the preacher. I could only stand up when our intrusive neighbour allowed me to do so. In all, it was a great night apart from the annoying distraction.

When we got home in the morning, I went straight to the kitchen and began cleaning and tidying up the house. I suddenly realised that I had cleaned and mopped for four hours at a stretch, and felt absolutely no pain, no discomfort! At no point did I have to stop to grab a seat half way through. I realised that God had healed my back and spine, and the swelling on my back had disappeared.

I was so happy to have been healed despite me not going out to the front to get prayed for! No one had laid hands on me! My God is a good God indeed! Blessed are those who put their trust in him. That was the end of an arthritic spine and any associated pain. Even when I have the odd pain come on, I know to tell it where to go, because I've been healed and set free from it. Glory to God!

Life was good despite our challenges. We were involved in ministry and other church activities. Our relationship with God was the most important thing to our family and that has not changed. We still hold the tradition of praying together whenever we're all home together. We fast regularly and take it in turns to prepare and pray. We are a musically inclined family, and some of us are still learning to play a musical instrument (well not naming names)!

I love going to the gym whenever I can get round to it. When my routine was set, I could sometimes go up to three to four times a week. I had gone for an aerobic exercise class this particular day and decided to use the machines before the class started. As I was on the trade mill sweating it out, I looked out at the sky as the tread mill was positioned by the window. I saw a collection of white clouds that looked like and angel with wings in a flying position! I was fixated on this picture in the sky, trying to make sense of it. It might sound funny but as I was analysing this, I felt a nudge in my spirit to leave, get out of the gym and go straight home. It was an urgent feeling that I couldn't describe.

I stopped the tread mill, picked up my bag and headed home.

When I pulled up on the drive, I noticed Charlie's car was there already, because he was due to have dialysis that day. I walked through the door, and I could see some of the items used to set up for dialysis treatment, scattered all over the place. I closed the door, looked up and saw Charlie sitting on the stairs. I called him but he did not respond. I shook him and called again, and this time he was startled as if he had just woken up from sleep.

"Charlie what's happened?" I asked.

"I don't know," he answered.

The history taking continued. "Did you fall? Did you bang your head?" I was asking all these questions but praying in tongues

at the same time. Thankfully I had peace, and it was as if I was taking directions from the holy spirit.

"Can you stand up?" I asked as I helped him up, and led him to the living room.

I ran upstairs and got the blood pressure machine, checked his blood pressure, pulse, respiration and oxygen saturation. All his para-metres were fine. He then asked me when I came in. That was when I knew that he had passed out on the staircase.

I offered him a glass of water which he drank and then he asked for another. I checked his observations again and everything was fine, but he looked tired. It wasn't long before his phone rang. It was his friend Niyi, so he began narrating what had happened to him.

He explained that he had picked up the things he needed for dialysis, and was carrying them up the stairs, when his leg suddenly became weak and gave way. Apparently that's all he could remember. He admitted to praying and asking God not to let him die alone in the house. He said he could feel himself drifting in and out of consciousness, and the next thing he knew he could hear me calling him. Once he had finished his phone call, we prayed and thanked God for saving his life.

We decided not to dialyse that night and have an early night instead. The devil failed woefully again. Our enemy will not triumph over us.

I really thank God for his faithfulness. I experienced first-hand the benefits of fasting and yielding to the Spirit of God. I was fasting that day, and it most definitely helped me receive directions from God's spirit with clarity and precision. If I had stayed in the gym, or panicked when I saw what had happened, I would have lost focus, and things would have played out differently. The Lord really does order the footsteps of his children.

> *The steps of a good man are ordered by the LORD,*
> *And He delights in his way.*

> Psalm 37:23

> *Trust in the LORD with all your heart, And lean not on your*
> *own understanding; In all your ways acknowledge Him,*
> *And He shall direct your paths.*

> Proverbs 3:5-6

I thank God for being in the driving seat. As a nurse my head knowledge would have told me to dial 999, but I dialled heaven instead and the one that does not fail, answered me and took over.

John 10:10 states:

> *The thief cometh not, but for to steal, and kill, and to destroy: I am come that they might have life and that they might have it more abundantly.*
> John 10:10

He gave Charlie life, and life to the full.

About a week after this incident, I experienced the worst day of my nursing career. I had gone out to see a patient and unfortunately when I got there, I found him dead. It was a planned joint home visit with his 88 year old sister, as she was concerned about his depressive episodes. She got there before me and had knocked on the door, but he wasn't answering. She'd seen him four days earlier and he was expecting us, and knew we were coming.

Eventually his sister used her own keys to open the door. When we went in, we called and called but there was still no answer. She went round the house and noticed that the kitchen door wouldn't open properly. We could see his breakfast cereal spilled on the floor, and his legs sticking out enough for us to see. We guessed he must have fallen. I was quite shaken up but had to pull myself together. I called the ambulance and the police and then informed my manager.

When the police arrived, they pushed the door right open. They immediately checked him and realised he had died about three days before the visit. He must have had a fall, and been unable to call for help, so died there on the floor. It was the worst day of my working life. I had the 88 year old sister to comfort and take care of, I had to give the police a report, and be there until the paramedics came and certified him.

Afterwards my manager called me and told me to go home from there, because I was very traumatised by the incident. I had called Charlie and told him what had happened, so he was at home waiting for me. It wasn't until I got home and I remembered what had happened to Charlie the week before, that it dawned on me what God had saved us from.

As I walked through the door, he held me and hugged me real tight. I sobbed and sobbed until I felt comforted a little bit. God is so awesome and the words of this song just came to mind. *When I think of the mercies of Jesus and all he has done for me, Almighty God hallowed be your name, your dominion is forever more. What can I say unto the Lord but to thank him for his mercies that never fail?*

And I will bring the blind by a way that they knew not; I will lead them in paths that they have not known: I will make darkness light before them, and crooked things straight. These things I will do unto them, and not forsake them.
Isaiah 42:16

CHAPTER 15

I WAS TROUBLED

It was 1999 and I had a worrying dream. In it I saw Charlie crying as he held up his ring finger for me to see, as he said, "I'm sorry." I also noticed that his ring was not on his finger. I began to search for it and when I found it I woke up. I was quite troubled about it and began to pray. I shared this with Charlie and shortly afterwards, he had the Leukaemia diagnosis. I thank God for healing him.

On the 01/04/2015 I had another dream. In it Uzoma ran to tell me that her dad had fallen. When I went to see what had happened, Charlie was sitting at the edge of Uzoma's bed in her room and crying. His teeth were a bit loose in conformity with old age. For a split second I remembered he was asleep, and I thought, *how did he get here?*

At that point I woke up and noticed he was still fast asleep by my side. I did not like this dream at all, and as I lay on the bed thinking about it, the Holy Spirit reminded me and clearly said:

"He's given me a garment of praise instead of a spirit of despair."

I got up and searched for it in the scriptures and it's recorded in: *Isaiah 61:3*

> *The oil of joy for mourning, The garment of praise for the spirit of heaviness; That they may be called trees of righteousness, The planting of the LORD, that He may be glorified.*
> Isaiah 61:3

I ended up reading the rest of the chapter which is very promising.

On the 15th/04/2015, I had another dream and I couldn't make head or tail of it and as I sat and pondered it, I heard *Romans 10:12*. When I woke up, I read the verse to the end of the chapter and this is what verses 12 and 13 says:

> *For there is no difference between Jew and the Greek: for the same Lord over all is rich unto all that call upon him. For whosoever shall call upon the name of the Lord shall be saved.*
> Romans 10:12-13

God was telling me something but I wasn't getting it. I didn't understand the message. This is what happens when we're so busy that we can't find the time, to even think and meditate on God's word. It can be the difference between victory and disappointment or success and failure. I have seen God's hand in my life countless times. Therefore my philosophy in life is that God will always give me the best, in any circumstance I find myself in. In fact my name

Chidinma means God is good and that says it all.

Charlie started losing weight and upon investigations, they found out that he had an overactive thyroid. They decided to operate on him and as this was going on, his immediate junior brother became very unwell. This was another cause of concern for us all.

While Charlie was in hospital recovering from surgery, I went to visit him one evening. When I got there, I saw an angel standing at the bed head of his hospital bed. The angel was a tall figure, his head almost touching the ceiling. He was clothed in white with wings, and he was smiling. I wasn't afraid at all but was filled with so much peace, as I tried to understand exactly what it was I was seeing. I stayed with Charlie while they prepared his discharge documents and medication. We got home, prayed and thanked God for his faithfulness.

Charlie was recovering very well and was supposed to be off work for two weeks. One evening during his dialysis session at home, he had a call from his junior brother Lawrence who said he didn't feel well at all. Soon after that conversation, we got the news that his brother was admitted into hospital. Naturally Charlie was troubled, so much so that he called me and sat me down. "I know that I'm not supposed to drive. I'm asking you to please grant me your blessing however, to go and see my brother tomorrow. I need to spend some time with him."

I knew he was worried and I didn't want to deny him that opportunity of seeing his brother. From a medical point of view however, I knew he shouldn't be going anywhere when he still had stitches in, and was still recovering from surgery. I therefore offered to come with him but he refused, so I gave him my blessing. I thank God that I did because a few days later, his brother Lawrence died.

His brother's death affected him badly and took a lot out of him. They had been so close all through their lives. They attended the same schools from primary school to university. They both studied medicine and specialised in exactly the same thing. There was never a day that they didn't speak to each other. They discussed medical practise, family, faith, friends, politics, absolutely everything.

In fact if I was walking past, and realised it was Lawrence on the other end of the phone, I knew I'd have to be patient.

Whenever they spoke, neither of them would be in any hurry whatsoever to finish the conversation. It was Lawrence who had donated his bone marrow to Charlie when he'd needed it. If the connection had been close before, the transplant just brought them even closer to one another.

Charlie was really hurt by his passing and took it very badly. He was almost depressed. He lost a lot of weight within a very short space of time. He wasn't eating like he used to, he was quiet and very withdrawn. It took him a while to recover from the loss, but eventually he did. After sometime, he regained some of the weight he'd lost, and started feeling more like himself. Slowly things improved and were looking up again.

On the 5th of December 2014 a Friday night, I was coming back from work, and was involved in an accident. I was hit by another vehicle as the other driver went through a red light. The impact was on the driver's side and that resulted in my right hand being knocked off the steering wheel, and my right leg forced off the brake pedal. The car spun round three times and eventually stopped by a small tree on the central reservation of the road. The contents of the car scattered all over the place and all I kept saying during this ordeal was, "help me Lord, help me Lord!" He didn't just help me but he saved my life.

I was quite shaken up and people came running to the scene. God sent a driving instructor (who was driving behind me at the time), to witness what had happened. He had some students in his car, and I'm sure that it was a good lesson for them.

He told me what to do because I was very clearly dazed, and didn't know what to do at the time. He advised me to call the police which I did. They were however too busy to come out to the scene of the accident, because it was one of their busiest nights. As there were no life threatening issues except car damage, the police advised us to exchange details and let our insurers sort it out.

While this was going on, Charlie called me to find out where I was because it was getting late. When I explained what had happened, he wanted to come and get me. I discouraged him however because I was about to start heading home anyway. After much persuasion he agreed to wait, and shortly afterwards I arrived home safely, thank God. There was not a scratch on my body, although I was very shaken up.

As I pulled up on the drive, Charlie was in his car about to drive to meet me at the scene. He stepped out of the car, stared at me for a while and then he hugged me. He said what he always said to me openly all the time. "Even though I've had my life flash before my eyes several times, I'm begging God to please allow me to go home first, whenever we come to the end of our time on earth. I would not be able to cope if you were to go to be with the Lord before me," he confessed.

"Stop that line of thought now Charlie, because our lives and times are in God's hands," I replied. I reminded him of what he once told me when we were young, that he would live to the age of eighty and we laughed about it.

The following day after the accident, I woke up with a severe headache that I'd never had before. There was pain in my arms and legs also. It turned out that I had sustained a severe whip lash injury. I had torn ligaments and tendons and there was fluid trapped in my muscles, so I was being investigated for these injuries. This took me out for weeks, but so long as we had each other, we were fine.

Although Charlie was regaining his weight, in February the medical team wanted him to have a full body scan and when the result came back, everything was fine. It dawned on him that he needed to pull himself together, and grieve with hope as a child of God.

One day during a home dialysis session, I noticed that the left side of Charlie's face was a bit swollen. I asked him about it and he said he had noticed it, but kept quiet because he was hoping to figure out what it was, while he prayed about it. Within days, certain words were becoming difficult for him to pronounce, and the contour of his face had changed. We remained in prayer and during one of the prayer sessions, as I laid hands on his face to pray, I felt the swelling move. We trusted God that it was going to go away.

When he went for his renal appointments, he mentioned it and was referred to the (ENT) Ear, Nose and Throat department. After an examination, he was told it was a parotid tumour which could easily be taken out. He was reassured that the success rate is quite high, and most of the time it is benign. Before he could be operated on however, they decided to scan him again and this was six months after the full body scan, he had already had. I was personally feeling for him with all the investigations and blood tests that he was being subjected to. This was apart from his kidney functions which were impaired but stable.

All the investigations came back normal, but they still wouldn't leave him alone. As a matter of fact on one occasion, I asked him to decline any more but he didn't listen to me.

The preparations for some of the investigations were quite rigorous.

It involved taking some solutions the night before, being without food for a period of time, and even drinking specific amounts of water. The aim was to clean out the intestines and make it easy for the scan to pick up any abnormalities. All this made him weak and tired and he still had to dialyse. My heart really ached to see what he was going through, so I decided to follow up on the enquiry I had made a while ago. It was to be screened as one of the donors to support Charlie, and hopefully cut down on the Kidney transplant waiting time. Our children were also ready to do the same for him.

Charlie was such a brilliant dad. He put the children in their place without thinking twice. He also showered them with so much love, mentored them and was their friend too. The boys confided in him about certain issues, which he would mention to me later on.

As his family he didn't want us to go that far for his sake, but we were happy to. I had collected the forms, read through the notes and was completing the form, when in a dream I heard the instruction to wait. I slowed down the momentum then, because I felt restrained but I continued praying about it, and believing God for a creative miracle.

I also joined up with my prayer group and family, to intercede for a miracle. At the same time we thanked God for life. I believe it's all about being able to discern the times, and as we know, God's time is the best in everything, and we also know that he is never late.

On the 14th of August during one of my quiet moments, I began to remember some of the words God had given me in recent months, and years concerning Charlie, and felt uplifted. Here are some of them: *Isaiah 61:3* which is stated earlier.

> *And I will bring the blind by a way that they knew not; I will lead them in paths that they have not known: I will make darkness light before them, and crooked things straight. These things I will do unto them, and not forsake them.*
> Isaiah 42:16

> *Remember the former things of old: for I am God, and there is none else like me, declaring the end from the beginning, and from ancient times the things that are not yet done, saying My counsel shall stand, and I will do my pleasure:*
> Isaiah 46:9-12

Also *Psalm 121*, my favourite Psalm.

I knew God was telling me something, but needed to set time apart to seek him concerning these words. Things were moving really fast, and my head was full. However in all these things, we never lost our peace. Yes, a part of me was yearning to get a clear picture of what was going on. All I knew to do was to trust God, and keep on trusting Him. To lose focus, would have been too costly and a failure for me, and that was a thought I wasn't prepared to entertain.

Throughout all of this, I was still in full time employment, and being very busy at work didn't help, but God gives us so much grace for each challenge. Charlie decided to stay off work for a few days, until he got a more clear picture of things, including treatment options.

When we went for one of the appointments, the picture painted wasn't good at all. I remember sitting there listening to the consultant, as he talked about the prognosis, giving predictions on how long Charlie had left to live! I was so stirred up as he spoke, because I knew it was not in the hands of man to determine what happened in our lives. I wasn't going to entertain any fear, because I knew the greater one lived in us. No matter how bleak the picture, God always has the final say in our lives. Not man.

So as the doctor continued discussing things, I was praying under my breath and rejecting every negative word spoken over Charlie. We'd been here before and through challenges in the past. God brought us through then, and I knew he hadn't changed and would certainly do the same again if we let him.

The consultant was very good and professional, and I knew he was just doing his job and carrying out his duties. As Christians however I knew that we should take authority over our lives, and declare what we want to see, rather than what we are told.

He asked questions which we didn't want to dwell on at the time. "Was Charlie misdiagnosed? Was it missed? How is it that six months ago, he had a full body scan which didn't show anything sinister, and now suddenly he is being given a diagnosis of advanced Parotid Cancer," he asked, seeming genuinely confused. Charlie told the consultant that we were Christians, and the same God who healed him of Leukaemia fifteen years ago, would heal him again this time.

He was immediately referred to another consultant who would be treating him, who also happened to be a Christian!

After discussing the treatment options, Charlie repeated the same words he'd spoken to the other consultant, that God would see him through. We had tasted the goodness of the Lord in many ways, and were determined not to entertain any doubts whatsoever.

In our quiet moments, I encouraged him to be strong and to not entertain fear. I did this because I knew that no matter how strong we are, our faith could be shaken. This was especially true being in the same profession, and understanding with clarity the diagnosis given and the severity of it! It was a whole new level of difficulty, hearing these negative declarations being made over and over. Every time we heard them, we constantly had to fight them off!

Proverbs 3:5-6 says:

> *Trust in the LORD with all your heart, And lean not on your own understanding; In all your ways acknowledge Him, And He shall direct your paths.*
>
> Proverbs 3:5-6

We literally lived this scripture. Although we were both in the medical field, we trusted God with all our lives and prayerfully made our decisions. We endeavoured to walk the path we felt God was leading us through. We didn't always get it right, but you live and learn from your mistakes. This time however, it was God's way not ours.

When we got a picture of what was happening, Charlie invited all our children home and told them the news. It was very difficult with lots of tears, unexplained silence, enquiring and probing looks and dull moods. We had to reassure them that all would be well. For them it was no doubt a feeling of deja-vu, accompanied by flash backs from fifteen years ago, and all that we went through then.

Thankfully we had grown in our walks with God, and had become more mature in our faith, to know that with God all things are possible!

Some of our family members, very close friends and church family were aware of the latest news. I also contacted a prayer group that I was part of called the Kabod prayer ministry, to ask people to join us in prayer. We didn't tell my mother, because we didn't want her to worry too much. It wasn't long however before she figured out that all wasn't well.

There were times in the past where I told Charlie not to leave me. He always looked at me and replied, "I am not going anywhere!"

I wasn't in any doubt at all, but it was my way of hearing him say it. I needed him to tell me those reassuring words that I loved to hear. When I told him not to leave me this time however, he replied, "It is not in my hands, but the same God who saw me through the last time, will do it again!"

On the 27th of August 2015, Charlie started the first chemotherapy treatment. The plan was that if his body responded well, then surgery might still be considered. The focus for the time being, was on the cancer treatment and his dialysis. That day we came back home after the treatment, in time for bible study at our house. Although he was very drowsy, he joined in and contributed to the discussion. When the bible study ended, and it was time to go to bed, I noticed he was taking his time.

His birthday was three days away, so my daughter Uzoma and his niece Uche had come home especially to celebrate with us. The boys were to join us also the following day. When he got up to go upstairs, I noticed he was quite weak. He did however insist I go first, and then he would follow, walking up the stairs behind me. I didn't argue and he walked up the stairs quickly. Once he got to the bedroom, he threw himself on the bed, and I could see that he wasn't himself at all. I began to pray in the spirit and asked the girls to dial 999 immediately.

He didn't like what I did and thought I was worrying too much, but I knew he needed to be checked out. I could see he was fighting against the effects of the drugs, that had been pumped into him earlier.

The ambulance crew checked him over, and all his parameters were alright except his oxygen saturation. Since he had only just had Chemotherapy (earlier that day), they advised that the best line of action would be for him to be observed in hospital overnight and we complied. At about 23:45pm that night, we headed to the hospital in the ambulance. While in the ambulance, Charlie was cracking jokes and he asked the ambulance crew their names, which they gladly gave. They were simply brilliant and very professional all the way through. Later on when I asked him why he wanted the names of the ambulance crew, he said it was because he intended to write to thank them for a job well done.

We didn't stop praying together, making declarations of the word of God, as well as speaking life over his health, despite the fact that we were in hospital. The word of God is an incorruptible seed, and will accomplish the purpose for which it was declared. What I'm about to tell you was probably one of the most challenging things, I've ever had to face in my whole life.

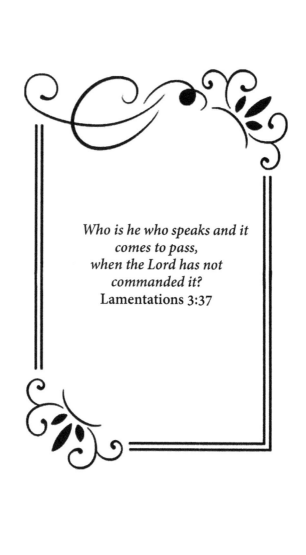

Who is he who speaks and it comes to pass, when the Lord has not commanded it?
Lamentations 3:37

CHAPTER 16

WE WRESTLE NOT AGAINST FLESH AND BLOOD

When we got to the hospital, Charlie was seen by one of the registrars who told us straight away, that he will be transferred to the ITU. The moment we got there, the real challenge began. There was such intense spiritual warfare going on, and you could literally feel the tension in the air and within me. The medical team took a look at his medical notes, and all they wanted to do, was to intubate him. They said it was because his oxygen saturation was low, and he was struggling to breathe. He was retaining a lot of fluid in his kidneys, because of the chemotherapy drugs he had been given earlier on that day.

The doctor said he was going to carry out some investigations and wanted me to give consent for Charlie to be intubated, if his results were grossly deranged. I however declined. Seeing his condition, I knew that if he was to be put on ventilator, that would be the end of him. He wouldn't be able to communicate and they could disconnect the machine whenever they wanted to. I thought I was in a movie but I wasn't, it was real! We had come from our home full of peace and joy, to this place of spiritual warfare where my husband was now, fighting for his life.

By the time the blood results came back, they were better than the medical team expected. They started him on a high dose of oxygen, and that helped his breathing but he could hardly say much. In the morning, the senior consultant in charge of ITU came to see him. He brought up the conversation again and kept talking about it all day. They put a lot of pressure on me, to consent to him being intubated (ventilated) but I refused. As a nurse, I know the importance of ventilators, but also the consequences and danger involved in using them.

My spirit was troubled because I could see what they were trying to do, and I wasn't going to let that happen. In their minds, they had already written him off because of his diagnosis. As far as I was concerned however, no one had the right to pull the plug on my husband. He became very anxious because he could hear everything they were saying, especially as his bed was just by the staff station. He was however unable to speak for himself. As a doctor he knew all the coded language they were using.

Each time they decided to intubate him, his test results normalised and this happened about three times over the course of three days.

I did not leave his bed side, unless there was someone who could contact me straight away if necessary. I only left him when I needed to have a shower and change my clothes. Afterwards I would come straight back to hospital. I had absolutely no desire for food because my appetite had dried up.

I was called in for discussion with the medical team several times, and it was just to try and persuade me to consent to intubation/ventilation. I got so fed up with the constant pressure they tried to put on me, that I even requested for a transfer to the Queen Elizabeth Hospital, where he was well known. They however refused to transfer him, stating that he wouldn't make it to QEH!

There was this particular doctor who came over to Charlie and started asking him totally irrelevant questions! "I hear you're a doctor, where did you study medicine? Where do you work?" he kept asking on and on.

I called these questions irrelevant, because he could see that Charlie was struggling to breathe, and had an oxygen mask over his face. He still persisted with his marathon style questioning, and expected him to respond at the same speed. It was even more surprising that he strangely seemed to find it all funny. I had to ask him to leave and come back some other time, when Charlie was feeling better and would be happy to answer all his questions then.

As a child of God, I had all my spiritual antennas up. The scripture says that we fight not against flesh and blood. I saw that encounter as satanic provocation and distraction. I knew that the best way to deal with such people, is to go to the place of prayer and contend with the spirit behind such actions, which I did.

The following day was Bescot market outreach day. I knew that I ought to be there, but also knew my place was by my husband's side. The Holy Spirit persuaded me to go, so I discussed it with Charlie, who also told me to go. He knew we had to mind our heavenly Father's business and that when we do, he will mind ours too.

I got my niece to sit with him while I went on the market evangelism outreach. I had some bible affirmations that I'd been reading and declaring over him, and I asked her to carry on declaring them over him while I was gone. Within three hours, I was back at the hospital.

Charlie's birthday finally came, and the children and grandchildren had come home to be with him. They had baked, cooked and gotten things ready to visit him in hospital and make his day special. When they arrived however, there was commotion because I was summoned yet again, and put under pressure to sign the consent form. I refused because I still had lots of questions. "As his breathing was already difficult, why put him on the ventilator? Would it mean switching off the machine if they weren't getting the desired results they wanted? Why wouldn't they dialyse him, since that would get rid of all the toxins that had built up in his body from the chemotherapy?" I asked.

What they did have was a cleansing machine rather than a dialysis machine which didn't help. When the consultant responded to my questions, he told me that they would switch it off if they needed to. That confirmed my suspicions.

He gave me that evening to make a decision, because I told him I needed to speak to my children about it. After the discussion, I was   sitting by my husband's side, when the same registrar that was asking the irrelevant questions came back with a nurse. He wanted to know if I had made a decision. There were no curtains drawn, his voice was raised and everyone could hear him. I told him I was waiting for my family to come, but he wanted me to give him an answer immediately. He said that if Charlie deteriorated he wanted a plan in place. I explained that I had just finished discussing with the consultant, and he was planning to see me for my decision, later on that day. The registrar ignored what I said, and carried on pestering me. At this point other patients and relatives were watching and listening. In the end I told him, "we will cross that bridge when we get to it." I will cross the bridge for you," he responded threateningly, at the top of his voice.

He rallied the nurses and started giving them instructions. When I walked past the room, I heard him mention Charlie's name. As I left the ward, my sons came in to stay with their dad as the number of visitors allowed was limited. I went outside and I wailed and cried my heart out to my heavenly Father. I asked him to step into this situation and help me. I looked up to him the one from where my help comes from. He is the Lord who made heaven and earth.

I then contacted Charlie's senior brother Etofolam Felix Osuji, and told him what was going on. I had come back upstairs at this point. The nurse came to take some blood to help them confirm things, for their planned course of action and guess what? His bloods were normal again! My God is truly an awesome God. He heard my cry. In the midst of the heat of all this, some of my husband's trusted friends turned up, as well as my children, and my brother. Our presence was felt and we were a force to be reckoned with, in the spirit. Dr Sam went in with Pastor Veronica and they prayed for him and anointed him with oil.

Within hours things began to change. Charlie was brighter and was actually now able to speak a few words. By the next morning, the 'death team,' had gone home and another team had taken over. The new consultant in charge that week, told me that he wouldn't have intubated Charlie.

He also said he was not going to be following this line of action. That was so reassuring to hear and more proof that the Lord answers prayers!

I had gone home for a shower and change of clothes the next day, when I got a call from the renal team. They asked about Charlie and when I narrated what had happened, the renal nurse specialist reassured me that someone would soon ring me back.

Within an hour, the QEH had contacted the hospital where Charlie was staying, to inform them that a renal consultant was coming out to review him. Before I could get back to hospital, the renal consultant had already been to see him, secured a bed for him at the QEH and planned a transfer for him the following day.

Charlie asked me to please go home and cook him a meal so that we could celebrate what God had done. The Lord came through for us and the next day, he was safely transferred to the QEH and for me it was a great victory.

In the book of Lamentations 3:37 it says:

> *Who is he who speaks and it comes to pass,*
> *when the Lord has not commanded it?*
> Lamentations 3:37

Our God is near to all who call upon Him, and to all that call upon Him in truth. As Christians we know that we do not wrestle against flesh and blood, but against principalities, against powers, against the rulers of the darkness of this world, against spiritual wickedness in high places. We see this in hospitals and certain institutions a lot.

I refused to be intimidated or bullied into making a decision. Instead I cried unto my Abba Father, and he heard me and intervened. God stepped into our situation and helped us. Hallelujah! If we had stayed any longer in that hospital, it would have been a different story at this stage. Our God had a different plan. At the time, things had been so bad, that Charlie sat me down by his bed side one night, before he was transferred. "You know I love you very much, but I don't like what you are going through. Please let me go!" he said.

I was shocked that he said that to me, and knew he said that from a position of fear and not of God. I therefore reminded him of what he had said to the children and to me, that the same God who saw him through the first time, will see him through again. I also reminded him that I had a covenant relationship with him through marriage. I told him that I knew that God wasn't through with him yet. So, I said NO to his request to let him go.

I knew why he was thinking that way. It was because he had never found himself in a situation where he couldn't speak for himself. I believe it was also all the negative reports, they had been spewing out that had begun to get to him. Thankfully I knew my husband well and was prepared to fight for him. We continued to pray and sing and make bible declarations by his bedside. I'm sure the enemy had planned to take him out, but my Jesus had already fought the battle and won, so we are more than conquerors in every situation. If they had considered dialysing him as a priority, rather than wanting to intubate him straight away, things would have been a lot better for us during that time.

The night before he was transferred, I had a meeting with the Nursing sister who wanted to hear my point of view. She wanted to know how she could help make the remainder of Charlie's hospital stay, a stress free one. I explained to her that Charlie and I were not strangers to the medical practice, and we knew what the values of the hospital were as stated in bold print. I confessed that what we couldn't understand was why some ITU (Intensive Care Unit) staff wanted to do things differently.

It was a good meeting and she was very apologetic, and made sure we got what we wanted during her shift. Some people had advised me to make a complaint, but I refused because we had forgiven them and I wasn't going to be distracted. We needed to remain focused in prayer. Charlie was still unwell, and it would have made no sense to start chasing trivial things and waste energy. Besides it would have been too painful to re-live. Such things create openings for roots of bitterness, pain and anger to creep in and we were not going down that route at all.

We always let God fight our battles and he did, so going back to complain and follow that path would not be glorifying to God. It was all a distraction. There's a proverb in my Ibo language that says, "if your house is on fire, you don't go about chasing rats." Looking back, I'm so glad we took that approach, because it would have been a wasted pursuit.

At the QEH, Charlie was treated with so much dignity and care and things started to get better. After a few weeks they were thinking of discharging him, but needed to put things in place to support us at home. We were told things weren't great but we had the right team of professionals around us. Some of the doctors and nurses were Christians and they took care of me too. They provided me with a mattress and clean sheets each night. I did not sleep at home all throughout his stay in these hospitals. Altogether that amounted to five weeks altogether. Charlie did not want me out of his sight, and I couldn't think of anywhere else I would rather have been.

We had prayers, communion and worship music on all the time. We had time to catch up and reflect on things. Our family and close friends visited regularly. There was always laughter coming from his room. I was going to work from visiting him at the hospital, and then back to him after work. I had fantastic work managers who supported me during this very trying time. I pray God will remember and bless them whenever it is their time of need.

On one of the nights when Charlie couldn't settle, he asked me to come and sit by his side. He began telling me how sorry he was, and how bad he felt seeing all I was going through at the time. He told me that he had asked God to forgive him for any sin in his life that may have resulted in the challenges we were facing. I quickly reassured him that it wasn't because of anything he had done, but rather an attack of the enemy on his health. I reminded him that Jesus had already paid for all our sins, and healing is available to us. The fact that we were still in hospital does not mean that God has not heard our prayers. We shared scripture, broke bread and prayed. Things were really looking much better, and he was looking forward to coming home.

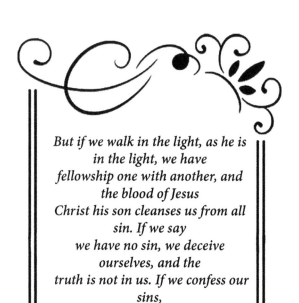

But if we walk in the light, as he is
in the light, we have
fellowship one with another, and
the blood of Jesus
Christ his son cleanses us from all
sin. If we say
we have no sin, we deceive
ourselves, and the
truth is not in us. If we confess our
sins,
he is faithful and just to forgive us
our sins and to cleanse us from
all unrighteousness.
1John1:7-9

CHAPTER 17
THE VISITATION

Charlie would ask me to make his favourite dishes. During this time he had developed a craving for cheese, so I teased him and said that we would open up a cheese factory when all this was over.

A few days later, Charlie called and woke me up from the floor where I was lying, and he asked me to sit by his side again. This time however he wasn't lamenting, but he wanted to give me instructions on what he wanted me to do, like someone who was about to leave.

He also told me where things were and so on. I didn't take it well and became very upset. I asked him why he was talking in this manner and where he thought he was going. I left him and went to the rest room. This was a concerning development I didn't like, and I wasn't happy about it at all. My faith was unshakable and even in the face of some obvious changes, I chose to believe what the word of God says. I know Charlie believed too, but as he was struggling with his breathing and having to ask people to do things for him, the situation worried him a lot.

I did most of the nursing care for him and the nurses issued his medication and other specialist treatment. We carried on with the faith proclamations, worship music and bible readings, and declared these things over him. Whenever I wasn't there and had to ask someone else to sit with him, I asked them to do the same.

I had lost a lot of weight because I went days without remembering to eat, or sleep. There were times I fell asleep at the traffic lights, and even when I was on the phone to people. It honestly took the strength and peace of God to get through it all.

I knew this fight wasn't against flesh and blood and that we weren't alone. God was on our side and there were people praying for us.

Since giving my life to the Lord, I had disciplined myself to live a fasted life and on this particular Friday, I decided to wait on the Lord. I was on duty and had to travel about twenty five miles to work and back. As I travelled back that night, I prayed and cried all the way. I told God that the weight of things was getting too heavy for me to bear. I confessed this was especially true with the conversations I'd been having with Charlie lately.

Before I got back on to the ward, I made sure I wiped my eyes as if nothing had happened. The last thing I wanted was for Charlie to find out I was upset. We stayed up chatting until we both fell asleep. In the early hours of Saturday morning, the Lord gave me a vision of a man standing by my husband's bed side. He was clothed in white with his hands spread out and I quickly recollected myself. I was joyful that God had sent his angel to come and visit him. I was convinced this meant he was going to come home soon. I pondered this in my mind, and prayed with so much hope and excitement. The weekend was a good one and we had close friends and family come to visit us. When we're believing God for a miracle, we need to be careful who comes around us, and who we allow to speak into our lives.

A friend of Charlie came to visit and started asking him whether he was on painkillers. He told him that he shouldn't be afraid to ask for more if he wanted. I quickly interjected and told him that Charlie wasn't in pain, but that if he was we would ask for some. This friend however wouldn't leave the matter alone, and kept on reminding him to ask for it. We knew that Charlie had been prescribed painkillers, but he wasn't in pain and didn't need them at that time.

Something funny happened that night. When the night nurse came round with the medication trolley, she asked if he was in pain and he said no, but he would like painkillers anyway to help him sleep better. I knew immediately that it had to do with what his friend had suggested to him. I pleaded with him and eventually he decided not take as much as he had asked for initially. That night, he was so restless but settled eventually and this was the effect of the medication he'd had. I believe that there is the need to guard our hearts at all times. Our eyes, ears and where we go are the gateways to our hearts. We therefore need to protect ourselves from contaminants and negative influences. We have to guard our hearts for out of it flow the issues of life.

> *Keep your heart with all diligence,*
> *For out of it spring the issues of life.*
> **Proverbs 4:23**

On Monday morning, the medical team informed me that there was going to be a meeting the following day at 3pm. (I did attend several of these during our stay in this second hospital as well). They weren't usually good reports, but respectfully I attended. I always rejected every negative word spoken over him or about him, praying under my breathe in tongues. Thankfully my spirit was on very high alert, as I was determined not to let the enemy creep in and spoil our testimony.

In the evening of that day, he was very bright and cheerful, cracking jokes as usual. He asked me to go and get him some cheese from the shops on the ground floor of the hospital. He enjoyed that and shortly afterwards he had his night medications, but he became restless. This time it was different and I held him in my arms and asked Uzoma to pull the red cord. The medical team came in and began to treat him. I was asked to leave the room but at first I refused, because

I wanted to be with him. However out of respect and to allow them space to care for him, I stepped out of the room.

I called family and close prayer partners and asked them to intercede fervently for Charlie, then I went back into the room where he was. The same room that had been full of medical staff, was now empty with just a male nurse standing at the door. He told me that the moment that I left the room, Charlie went into a deep sleep.

They had given up on him but I wasn't going to give up on him. I called my daughter who was very tearful at this time, and we began to sing choruses. I also read words of scripture over him.

After a while, I called Charlie three times and on the third time he answered me and asked where he was. He also asked for some water. The nurse who was standing at the door and watching, shouted out with excitement. "Madam you are very powerful," he commented.

I corrected him and told him it had nothing to do with me, but we serve and worship a living God.

He quickly checked Charlie's parameters, and all his observations were perfect. The nurse turned round and looked at us in amazement, admitting that he couldn't believe what he was seeing. He did confess that they thought it was over, and he was just standing around earlier to know when Charlie would breathe his last breath, so that he could record it. Our God is wonderful and awesome in power.

When Charlie drank that water, he asked for another glass and the swelling on his face had disappeared, and his swollen legs had come down. It was as if he had just been sleeping. I told him how he scared us all, but he just opened his eyes, looked at me briefly and then went back to sleep. I sat and watched him as my daughter had to go off to work from there as she had planned to do.

At breakfast time, Charlie told me that he was hungry so I fed him and then he went back off to sleep. At that time I began to feel unwell. I started shivering and as I sat by his side I fell into a very deep sleep. Suddenly I woke up and the environment in the room had changed, so much so that you could hear a pin drop. The room was very quiet and airy and there was definitely something about it which I couldn't explain. I quickly jumped to my feet and checked Charlie out. He was still sleeping peacefully, so I picked up my phone and began again to read the bible affirmations over him.

When he did wake up he asked for food again, so as it was lunch time, I got his food and fed him. It wasn't long afterwards the medical team called me for the usual meeting. It wasn't a good meeting because they basically told me to prepare for the worst. They even confessed that they were surprised he was still even with us. In response I asked them whether they had ever seen a miracle before. Some of them said yes, while others said no. I challenged them and told them to be prepared to see one. I thanked them all for their care, dedication and professionalism. I then left the room and hurried back to Charlie's bedside. I had to hold myself together, and began to prayerfully read the affirmations over him.

CHAPTER 18

THE GLORIOUS EXITS

When I got back to Charlie's bedside, he asked me where I had gone. I explained that I had been called in for another meeting. He asked me to adjust his pillows and then we began reading again. He said Amen to each of the readings and affirmations. He asked me where the cool breeze was coming from. I couldn't feel any, but asked if he wanted the window closed. He declined, telling me that he was enjoying the coolness of the room.

I carried on reading again, and as I held his hand he suddenly squeezed mine tightly three times. I was about to ask him what was going on, when Uzoma walked through the door and asked how he was. I was giving her an update, when I noticed that his head was tilted to the left side. I called him but this time there was no response. He was gone. It was as if he was waiting for our daughter to come into the room, before he existed to glory.

We cried out again for help, but this time it was to confirm the obvious. We were crying, but I was still reading the bible over him at the same time, panic and hysteria literally taking over. My daughter and I sat there for another five hours, praying and hoping he would ask me for a drink again or call my name, but he didn't this time. Not this time. He was really gone. My Charlie was gone.

To say that going back home that night without him was difficult is an understatement. I was crushed, torn and totally grief stricken. This was tough as I now had the responsibility of taking care of our children and grandchildren, and being strong for them. My world had turned upside down. Many times I sat hoping that someone would wake me up from this nightmare. It was however real and my soulmate was gone. During this time, I came to realise how blessed we were with wonderful families and friends, and their support and love was exceptional. My children tried to be strong but it was too much to bear. The news broke them. Their dad, hero and mentor had gone.

As we struggled to come to terms with our loss, my niece Oge, who had been battling lymphoma also passed six days later. It was exactly one week after she turned twenty. It had to be a dream. Everything happened so fast. It saddened me that I wasn't there when she passed, but I was somewhat comforted that my youngest brother Oso and his wife were there with her.

Oge was full of life, fun to be with, so loving and full of humour. Although she was unwell, it didn't stop her at all from shopping and dressing up and being ever so cheerful. She even kept a journal and had planned to write about her experience when she was fully recovered. At one point she was even told she was in remission. She was a determined young woman and full of wisdom beyond her years.

I remember the mother's day message she sent me from her hospital bed. It moved me to tears, and made me realise that although our children are young, we should never ever take for granted the power of love, and the type of relationship we have with them. The things you do and say to them do make a huge impact.

In the text, she told me that I didn't have to run around her and shower her with gifts, to show my love for her. She said she could see my love for her in the way I related to her, and the quality of time I spent with her, rather than the things I bought for her. She was an absolute gem.

During her sickness, my brother, Nnanna and his wife Maureen and their children had travelled on different occasions from Nigeria to be with her. As a family, it was devastating to lose two members of my family within one week. The loss of a child is a whole new world of pain, so difficult to express with mere words, and I couldn't imagine what her parents must have been going through. To say it was a difficult time for my family is to put it lightly. We stayed trusting God, and the unity and love of our family sustained us all through that time.

I went to the registry office with my family to register Charlie's death and the lady asked a question which churned my stomach so bad, I felt sick. She asked loudly, "who is his widow?"

I immediately looked around and everybody was looking at me. There and then, it hit me that I had become a widow. The woman was actually referring to me. *Dear Lord, was this going to be my identity? Chidinma the widow?* I wondered to myself. I was determined not to let that define me. Although that decision didn't come immediately, it was a tough and necessary one.

My mother had been very close to my husband, they were like friends really and they always had so much to talk about, it was almost uncanny. I loved their relationship. Of all her grandchildren Oge had been the one that looked like her the most. When mum received the news of her passing, it was extremely heart breaking for her to say the least. As was typical of my mum however, she soldiered on and consoled me all the way through. She was the one that helped me to organise so many things back home, in preparation for Charlie's funeral, especially as his body was repatriated to Nigeria. She let my children know that their dad had gone to rest, after he had lived a wonderful life.

Her tribute for both funerals were documented in the programmes. On the week of the funerals, I noticed that my mother wanted everyone around her. She offered words of advice as she normally did, but she was noticeably very anxious about lots of things. I figured it was because she wanted everything to go well.

She was inconsolable but like every brave woman, initially she pulled herself together. When she arrived at my house in Nekede village, something had definitely changed about her. She appeared weak and nothing like the mother I had just seen days before. I thought nothing of it as she was still actively marshalling everyone to help me, and still offering words of advice on different things.

On the morning of my husband's funeral, I went to the room where she was staying with her friend and sisters, and she sat me down and reminded me that it was going to be a long and difficult day. She however encouraged me to be strong and put my trust in God. She also told me not to be bitter, but to thank God for healing Charlie when he had Leukaemia, many years before, giving him another fifteen plus years. She reminded me of all the things we witnessed, of the things God did during that time. She then prayed for me, and shared some words of wisdom and encouragement. The ceremony went well.

I sat down after the interment and stared into space. I spent time reflecting on things and wondered how to forge ahead with life without Charlie. During this time, I saw a vivid picture of a sunset in the sky. Immediately the Holy Spirit reminded me of the dream I had about ten years before, about a similar looking sunset. It troubled me at the time and I prayed about it, but eventually left it. When I saw the same sunset from my dream in the sky years later, peace flooded my heart.

I stared at it for a while with tears streaming down my face in realisation. The Lord had shown me all those many years ago what would be coming but I couldn't decipher it at the time! The truth is, I still have a lot of revelations I'm yet to figure out, but I know that I'll learn with the help of the Holy Spirit.

Two days after my husband was laid to rest, my mother passed as well. I remember after the outing service for Charlie, at Praise centre International Owerri, we headed to the hospital to see my mother.

I had left her bedside at the hospital early that morning, after she was admitted the night before, to get ready for Charlie's outing service.

I realised that so many people from the service wanted to come with us to visit her. I was trying to work out in my head, in what order we would visit her, so we didn't over crowd the ward. What I didn't realise, was that everyone except my children and I, all knew what had happened.

When we got to the hospital grounds and I saw my brothers and cousins, all coming towards me from different directions, I thought, *oh what a gathering, Mma will be happy to see us all.* That thought evaporated when I asked about her, and the only response I received from my brothers, was a long cold stare with glistening eyes. It dawned on me that my sweet mother had left me too.

At this time, I hoped the last few weeks was just a nightmare, but with this as well, the feeling of it being a nightmare didn't even come close. I felt pain in my soul, pain like I had never felt before. It was like being peeled like an onion with each layer stripped, till there was nothing left of me. I was numbed to a pulp, and life for me became like a vapour, meaningless and empty.

When we got home, I began to reflect on the events of the previous days and I heard from people what my mother had said repeatedly. Apparently she had made peace with God and was ready to go. She had also asked God for all her children to be around her in her final hour. When I heard this I knew she got her heart's desire, and it gave me some peace and comfort. Mma and Charlie were my best friends, my confidants and encouragers and they were gone.

My reaction was, "Ok Lord, what have I done wrong? Please tell me so I can repent of it." I felt completely lost, lonely, confused and my head was really messed up. At the same time, I knew I had to be strong for my children and grandchildren, my brothers and other family members. My mum and my husband left very big shoes that I certainly didn't know how to fill. One minute I was fearless in the face of adversity, the next I was vulnerable and in so much pain.

I became acquainted with grief which is definitely not a good thing. In my pain, I turned to the Lord for comfort. Many times I couldn't find the words to pray or sing, so I just knelt quietly before the Lord, hoping He'd hear my heart.

This went on for weeks until gradually I was able to begin to sing again. I joined my Kabod prayer group every morning, and the Holy Spirit continued to minister to me removing the pain and grief gradually.

I have deliberately left out so many things because the Holy Spirit asked me to write this book with victory as a focal point.

Today I celebrate the victorious journey that my family and I have been on, as God continues to bless us daily. I resolved that I wasn't going to ask God, 'why' because I know HE loves me, and nothing could ever separate me from His love. My conviction in life as I've mentioned time and time again over the course of this book, is that God will always give me the best at any point in my life. If I did ask him, I would have to go back and apologise.

In Romans 8:31-39 it says:

"What then shall we say to these things? If God is for us, who can be against us? He who did not spare His own Son, but delivered Him up for us all, how shall He not with Him also freely give us all things? Who shall bring a charge against God's elect? It is God who justifies. Who is he who condemns? It is Christ who died, and furthermore is also risen, who is even at the right hand of God, who also makes intercession for us. Who shall separate us from the love of Christ? Shall tribulation, or distress, or persecution, or famine, or nakedness, or peril, or sword? As it is written: "For Your sake we are killed all day long; We are accounted as sheep for the slaughter." Yet in all these things we are more than conquerors through Him who loved us.

For I am persuaded that neither death nor life, nor angels nor principalities nor powers, nor things present nor things to come, nor height nor depth, nor any other created thing, shall be able to separate us from the love of God which is in Christ Jesus our Lord."

Although I was in pain, the love of God was stronger than my pain. For my own peace of mind however, I told God I wouldn't ask why, but would like him to help me understand the events of the past few months. We loved God and served him passionately, even more so after he healed Charlie from Leukaemia, so I really wanted to understand.

I have since grown to have an intimate relationship with Jesus Christ, and now nothing is done out of the flesh. Instead I always seek God concerning things, wait till I get a green light before I proceed, regarding making decisions or doing things, much to the frustration of certain people who always ask, "Must you ask God everything?" and my response will always be "YES."

I don't always hear or receive guidance or direction straight away, and like every good soldier, you have to obey the last order until you receive a new direction. This has saved my skin a few times. God is not sitting on his throne and dishing out our requests as they come, no! He is our heavenly Father who loves us unconditionally. He is relational and wants fellowship with us, so we have to trust Him and be patient. If the outcome is not good, then it's not from God. He is the God of the mountain and the God in the valley of life. When things go wrong, he'll make it right.

I knew at this point that Charlie wasn't going to walk through the door, much as sometimes I did wish he would. I knew also that I will never be alone. I belong to Jesus, and he is more than able to take care of my children and I. He is the husband of the widow and a father to the fatherless.

For we know in part and we
prophesy in part.
But when that which is perfect
has come, then that
which is in part will be done
away. For now we see
in a mirror, dimly, but then face to
face. Now I know in part, but then
I shall know just as I also
am known.
1 Corinthians 13:12

CHAPTER 19

GOD IS ALL KNOWING

I immersed myself in the word of God as that was the only thing that brought me comfort. During one of my reflective moods, the Lord answered my prayers, and gave me a word. He said to me, *"you only know in part."*

This is from *1 Corinthians 13:9-10 and verse 12* of the same chapter and it states:

> *For we know in part and we prophesy in part. But when that which is perfect has come, then that which is in part will be done away. For now we see in a mirror, dimly, but then face to face. Now I know in part, but then I shall know just as I also am known.*
> **1 Corinthians 13:12**

When I got this, I had so much peace and knew that God was telling me something. Although we had prayed and believed God for Charlie's healing, I believe he gave up too soon, was ready to go home, and eventually gave up fighting. Although I will not fully understand everything on this side of eternity, my prayer has been to

hold on tight to God, knowing that when my time comes (at a good old age), and I see Him face to face, he will make all things clearer to me. Truly I could only judge based on what I know, but my God is all knowing and HE will make it plain when I stand before HIM.

In the book of *Isaiah 42:16*

I will bring the blind by a way they did not know; I will lead them in paths they have not known. I will make darkness light before them, And crooked places straight. These things I will do for them, And not forsake them.

This path is definitely very unfamiliar, and it's by the saving strength and mercy of God, that we could come this far. I can also testify that God has fulfilled this scripture in my life, and I am still living it. Another scripture that has meant so much to us as a family is that, God never leaves us nor forsake us. As I have dwelt on this, I have drawn strength and comfort from Him.

One of our family friends who heard about my mum called me, and asked me a very difficult question.

"Sister Chidi, should I call you Job?" he asked.

"No, call me Chidi for my God is good indeed," I replied.

After that telephone conversation, I felt strongly to go and read the book of Job. When I did, it blessed me a lot and became integral and instrumental to part of my healing process. I could relate to some of his pain and how his friends treated him. I also know that when such things happen, most people mean well but words are like arrows, and can be very damaging. For instance, a few people made passing comments like, it was the thought of me that killed my mother because she loved me so much. That was very painful. I had to forgive them and let go, but I believe there's a better way to console people who are grieving. Always weigh your words and speak only what the Holy Spirit gives you for that person. Sometimes, just sitting in that person's company and saying nothing is even more therapeutic.

The word of God heals, Jesus is the word as it tells us in:
John 1:1-2:

> *In the beginning was the Word, and the Word was with God, and the Word was God. He was in the beginning with God.*

So when we begin to read the bible, we are communing with God and he will speak to us. Sometimes people have been healed and restored by just spending time reading the word of God. The Bible is not just an ordinary book, so when I began to read the book of Job, words came alive and brought me so much comfort.

> *I have heard of You by the hearing of the ear, But now my eye sees You. Therefore I abhor myself, And repent in dust and ashes.*
> Job 42:5-6

I read with so much interest that some days, I had to be reminded to eat. The more I read, the more I saw the hand of God in the life of Job and how he was restored fully. The word of God became my medicine, and gradually my joy was being restored. This is especially because we grieve with hope, knowing that we will see our loved ones again.

I knew it was time for me to arise from where circumstances had placed me, and look up to what God has planned and purposed for me.

The day I read *Job 14: 7-9*, my heart leapt for joy and it states:

> *For there is hope for a tree, If it is cut down, that it will sprout again, And that its tender shoots will not cease. Though its root may grow old in the earth, And its stump may die in the ground, Yet at the scent of water it will bud And bring forth branches like a plant."*

Although all these things have happened, there is hope because if God be for us, then who can be against us. He did not withhold his only Son Jesus, but through Him, gave us all things. Charlie may have gone to glory, but he left a huge legacy to our children. As long as God is on the throne he has promised to lead us and see us through. It is then that we will come through victoriously.

I began to see Charles in our children, their mannerisms, sense of humour and the joy they bring me every single time. I have always been friends with my children, but now they're even closer to me than ever before. It was time to rise and forge ahead with life, but I was very tearful and felt the loss and separation very deeply. That is alright because I know that, the glory and the lifter up of my head is always with me. The scent of rain for me, is the word of God and the Holy Spirit guiding us daily, leading us in triumphant paths. I was being revived and was determined not to let my circumstance define me. I began to prayerfully resist negative thoughts and feelings, and learned to take my thoughts captive.

I refuse to let my emotions dictate my life, so I had to constantly affirm the promises of God, and remind myself of God's goodness and all the blessings in my life. I saw God move miraculously on so many occasions. I began to speak life into situations that would otherwise have gone very badly. I began to see things turned around for our good. The word of God is life and indestructible, and once released with faith, it will accomplish the purpose for which it was sent. Therefore, speak life and effect changes in your circumstances and your world. God said, we should declare a thing and it shall be established.

I asked God to make me like Anna. She was widowed at a very young age, and spent her time fasting and praying that she will see the Messiah and the Lord granted her request. She was in the temple when Mary and Joseph brought Jesus to be dedicated as a baby. I decided to continue to live a fasted and yielded life, and I have seen God at work. Do I still cry? The answer is yes I do. Has it been smooth sailing? No it hasn't, but one thing I know is that I am never alone.

Galatians 2:20 states:

> *I have been crucified with Christ; it is no longer I who live, but Christ lives in me; and the life which I now live in the flesh I live by faith in the Son of God, who loved me and gave Himself for me.*

I am a product of grace and that's what's been keeping me, and I know that God still has plans for me.

Not by works of righteousness which we have done, but according to His mercy He saved us, through the washing of regeneration and renewing of the Holy Spirit, whom He poured out on us abundantly through Jesus Christ our Saviour.
Titus 3:5-6

CHAPTER 20

MY CHARIS JOURNEY

I was coming back from work one evening and as I walked to my car, I heard a mocking voice in my spirit, saying "the spring in your step is gone!" I quickly got into the car and cried all the way home. I went straight to my bedroom, knelt down and began to pray Then I heard another voice saying, *the spring in your step is not broken!*"

I finished my prayers, wiped my tears and enjoyed my evening meal.

God is the spring in my steps. He is with me, and I just want to tell you that life is spiritual. There's more to life than meets the eye, but we need to be in that place of prayer, to be able to decipher some of these things and hear God clearly. God loves us and wants the best for us. At this time, I began to reflect on the times I shared with Charlie,

and the things we had planned to do together. One of those plans was to go to bible college.

I pondered this in my mind and wondered how this was going to work because I was still in full time employment. On the 25th of November 2016, one of my friends who graduated from bible college some years back, and a staff member at Charis Bible College (CBC) called. They informed me that CBC was going to start Saturday Hybrid School in January 2017. She knew Charlie and I always wanted to attend and had made it part of our retirement plan. So I and another good friend of mine enrolled. That was how I started my Charis journey. I was still in full time work as a nurse, and about one year into a Masters degree programme in Advanced Clinical practice. However because, it was running for two Saturdays a month, it was alright for me. I knew that I would probably have limited time to myself, but it didn't matter because I saw this as an opportunity I wasn't going to miss.

In the Saturday school, there were so many professionals from different fields of life, and I felt right at home because we had so much in common. As a Christian I had grown to love the Lord, and love studying the bible. I thought I knew the bible until I went to bible college. It's not really about head knowledge, but about lives transformed and minds renewed.

I remember being told that the only text book we needed in the first year was the bible alone. As I sat and listened to the teachings, module after module, testimony after testimony, my heart was transformed. It wasn't because of anything I or anyone else did, but it was the power of the word of God.

It was effortless and reminds me of the scripture *in Titus 3:5-6* that says:

Not by works of righteousness which we have done, but according to His mercy He saved us, through the washing of regeneration and renewing of the Holy Spirit, whom He poured out on us abundantly through Jesus Christ our Savior.

Sitting under the word of God constantly, changed my life even when doing my assignments or tests, as I was still into the word of God.

When I went into Charis, I was in pain, broken and grief

stricken. Although that was my background at that time, I never lost my joy because Jesus is my source. HE is the embodiment of the Godhead, and in Him I am complete. This resulted in me being healed, renewed, transformed, and all this was completely effortless. I even had to wonder whether everything was right with me, but that's what happens when you dwell and abide in God's presence. All other things become insignificant in the light of God's glory and grace.

During one of the lessons, the Holy Spirit made it known to me that going to CBC (Charis Bible College) was the cement that brought it all together for me. I am still learning and haven't arrived yet, but I have taken off and I know that I'm on the right path. Putting blocks together will not build a house, but when you cement the individual blocks together, it leaves no room for unwanted creatures to come in. When you build a house and begin to decorate, you end up with an edifice and that's what the knowledge of the word of God does. I enjoyed my first year so much and I went on to do my second and third year.

This was one of the best decisions I've made in life and I couldn't have given Charlie a better legacy because, I did it for both of us. Everything I learned I will take with me to my household, ministry, friends, and wherever God takes me. Also Charles's name will always be mentioned, because it was our plan and I did it for us. I know he is looking down and smiling at the achievement.

Bible college gave me the opportunity to meet other like-minded Christians and to make lots of new friends. We always encouraged one another and straight away, I knew I was in a different environment. It was so refreshing because I didn't have to watch my back, or mind what I said all the time.

In August 2017, my second son Emeka Fredrick got married to Bianca in a beautiful and memorable ceremony. During the wedding, we had families and friends travel from far and near to attend, and I was grateful and happy about that. It was the first big family event after my husband's passing and it was tough emotionally. I had people around me, but felt the void that Charlie's death had left within me, and I felt very lonely. Although Charles wasn't there physically, I knew he was looking down and watching in admiration. I always remind myself that I have God the Father, God the Son and God the Holy Spirit with me always, so I'm never alone and God has surrounded me with a wonderful family, and friends who are like my own blood relatives.

A year later God added to my family another little star, Brielle Adaeze Osuji. I am truly a blessed and victorious woman. The devil isn't going to sit back and watch me cruise through life so, I know there will be challenges, and one of them has been an attack on my health. As I was coming back from work one day, the Lord showed me a vision of a little girl whose body was covered in spots. As I looked on, this little girl plunged into what seemed like a stream of water coming from a fountain. When she did, all the spots on her body lifted, and immediately this old song came to mind and I began to sing it all the way home. *"There is a fountain filled with blood drawn from Emmanuel's veins and sinners plunged beneath the flow and loose, all their guilty stains..."*

Well I wondered about the vision and didn't know who the girl was, so I continued to pray about it. Two days later when I was in bible college, during a lecture my heart was troubled. I began to think about a friend who was very ill with Cancer at the time, and I knew I needed to pray immediately. I told the Holy Spirit that when I stand up to step out of the class, whoever I met on my way out, I was going to ask to agree with me in prayer for my friend's healing.

As I stood up and turned to leave the class, the college director Ken Chang was right there and asked if I was ok. He followed me to the dining area where some of the staff were sitting. I shared with him the vision I had, and the burden that just came upon my heart and we prayed together for my friend. Then he began to pray for me too. I left it there and thought nothing of it. This happened on Saturday.

The following Tuesday as I drove to work, I began to feel really funny and as a nurse, I knew something wasn't right. I suddenly began to experience chest pain which started radiating to my left hand side, and I felt numbness on the same side. I was also sweating at same time. I couldn't stop driving because it was on a red route, so I began to pray for divine intervention and God answered speedily.

I got to work safely and carried on as if nothing had happened, until it began to happen again. This time I asked a colleague to check my blood pressure and my readings were off the scale, so I was sent home.

When I got home I crawled into bed and tried to rest, but my blood pressure wasn't coming down quick enough. Therefore the next day, I thought it best to go to the GP. When I did, there was a big panic. They knew me and all that had happened and didn't want to take any chances. They told me off for not coming straight to the surgery the day before. After all the tests and investigations, I was asked to go home and rest. I was also told that if I had another episode, then I must hurry to the hospital or dial 999. They started me on some medications and when I got home, I took them. I still headed out because I was meant to be at the university for lectures. It wasn't long after the lecture started, that the pain came back again. This time I was sent to the accident and emergency department with a suspected heart attack.

After six hours of tests, investigations and monitoring, I was told to go home and rest, because my troponin levels were normal after several repeated tests. I was however to come back if I felt any more chest pain. On three separate occasions within five days, I attended Accident and Emergency and on one occasion, as I sat there waiting to be seen, I asked myself what I was doing in hospital. *I shouldn't be here!* I thought to myself. At this point, I wanted to go home and as God would have it, I was sent home again.

During one of the appointments, the Lord told me as I left the hospital, that only He can heal a broken heart. I made a note of that and because I was asked to go home and rest, I spent all my time resting and reading the bible and it did me a lot of good.

CHAPTER 21
THE TURNING POINT

It was during this time that the Lord gave me another picture, of a man struggling to walk because he was carrying another man on his back. The one being carried, had his legs dragging on the floor. This made it hard for the one bearing the load to walk properly. Immediately the Holy Spirit said to me, *"that is you,"* and I knew it was time to make changes.

I went into nursing when I was eighteen years old, and have worked all the way through, from my training days to practicing in the Nursing profession. The only time I stopped work, was for my family to settle into work and school respectively. Altogether this amounted to about nine months altogether in about 40 years, apart from annual leave and maternity leave periods. Right there on my bed, I made the decision to reduce my hours at work with a view to retiring soon. I also decided to withdraw from the Masters programme but to continue with bible college.

Although my fees were being paid for to do the Masters programme, in bible college I had to pay my school fees. It was however an easy decision for me and I had so much peace because, my decisions were borne from a place of prayer. After three weeks of recuperating from a suspected heart attack, or (broken heart syndrome) as some people call it, I was ready to go back to work. The first thing I did, was to arrange a meeting in which I laid out my plans to my directorate lead. She was very understanding and I sincerely apologised for withdrawing from the Masters programme. I explained that I was ready to pay back any outstanding fees if I was asked to do so.

God gave me favour with that, but what I did not envisage was the attack at work. It dawned on me that I had to keep my spiritual antenna on at all times. The bible says that while men slept, the enemy came and sowed tares. As Christians, we need to be spiritually alert at all times. Remain focused and the Lord will see you through.

What I faced from a very small number of staff was cold treatment, malicious rumours and an attempt to manipulate things, which I would class as bullying and harassment. However I wasn't going to allow any weak minded people, to make my work life uncomfortable. Their actions were swallowed up by the wealth of love, friendship, joy and laughter, from a great number of other colleagues and that, was good enough for me.

I knew that everyone will not like me and that's fine, because I needed to be focused on Christ, and not on making people like me. I've never been a 'yes person,' but I always remind myself that I am an ambassador for Christ and I'm there to shine, cause a positive influence and to be a blessing. That was how I literally carried myself at work. I was determined to see the good in everyone, because no matter our differences, backgrounds and circumstances, there's a pearl in everyone, we just need to see them through the eyes of Christ.

One of the highlights of my Charis experience was going on a mission trip. Although I have always seen myself as a missionary in this country especially (when I'm at Bescot market), and built relationships with the team, forging friendships, sharing the love of Christ to the least, lost and marginalised, going to Athens topped it all for me. The enemy was out to stop me through attacks on my family's health and even bereavement, but as the saying goes when the world throws lemons at you, make lemonade out of it. I certainly did that, and all the rocks the enemy threw at me, I used to build an altar of praise to the glory of God.

We stayed focused on Christ and it has been a victorious journey. In every situation, we win because the greater one lives in us, and if God be for us, then who can be against us?

Travelling to Greece was a blessing, and it has been said that when you are going on a mission trip, whatever expectations you have, just lay them aside and allow the Holy Spirit to take the driving seat. The first reality check I got, was after the welcome and initial briefing, our host Pastor Stavus of Athens Christian Centre, (Ano Patissia the area where the church was located) announced that our hosts for the night were outside waiting for us. When we got outside we realised that there were no cars, and my host took the three of us on a fifteen minute hilly walk to her house, for the night before we checked into our hotel the next day. After the flight and road trip to the centre, the last thing my flesh wanted was to walk anywhere, but we were prepared for this and God was with us. The terrain in Athens is quite mountainous so it was a struggle initially, but we got used to it and enjoyed the walks all throughout our stay. About 80% of our journey was done on foot, so we lost a few pounds in weight, although the good food was enough to satisfy us after each day's activity.

As a football fan the 20 minutes train journey to Piraeus was pleasurable, because it gave me the opportunity to get a glimpse of the Olympiacos stadium which seats over 32,000 fans.

The trip to Athens was very impactful in many ways. We had the opportunity to go and help out in the immigration centres. This involved looking after children from a few months old to thirteen years, while their parents were being interviewed to get their immigration status situations sorted out.

At the Immigration centre, most of the people were from Afghanistan, Syria and Iraq. Listening to their stories moved and filled us with so much compassion. They had lost their homes, livelihoods and even families because of war, or ISIS invasion of their countries. Now they had ended up in Greece and were applying for ID Cards to enable them work and live meaningful lives. It was a joy to be with the children and to help them with colouring, writing, playing games, as well as offering them snacks, while their parents were being interviewed.

We went to the refugee centre to cook, feed hundreds of refugees, hear their stories and pray for them. In another refugee centre for men, the Christian brothers who went there came back with good reports of the teaching of the word of God. There were also testimonies from pastors who were once refugees from Muslim countries, who were now Christian pastors fired up for Jesus!

We spent a lot of time sorting out and arranging charity donations, of clothes from churches all over the world. These refugees depended on these gifts from churches, to be able to maintain their dignity and keep warm in the winter.

On one of the days, we went to a gypsy camp in an isolated desert near Thessaloniki. This camp had about 1,000 gypsies living there and as we approached, we were greeted with a sight one could liken to a refuse dump or flight tipping sight. There were pieces of broken bottles and used carrier bags littered everywhere. The area was surrounded by mountains, and the living conditions and life generally in this camp was dire. There was no water or electricity supply, and the only source of heating was a fire place with an improvised chimney they had built, which channelled the smoke into the open air.

Their homes were makeshift huts, made of pieces of glass, cardboard, and whatever pieces of corrugated iron sheets and wood, that they could find to build a shelter structure for themselves. They slept on the bare concrete floor with a few layers of blanket if they had them. Some of them hadn't eaten or showered for days. Things were pretty bad and that broke our hearts. Some of us couldn't hold back the tears, because of the living conditions they were forced to live in. They seemed to have been forgotten by the government.

Children had no source of education at all. The closest they got to a pen and paper was when Pastor Stavus and his team visited them, to give them food parcels and clothes. They spent time with the staff learning rhymes, drawing and colouring or engaged in one learning activity or another. Children as young as 12 years of age were married with their own children. It was a case of *'children having children!'*

The life in the camp was tough because of the high level of violence. Some of them had become Christians and the Pastors that went there had to solicit funds to build a church. This was however vandalised by some of the people at the camp, because some of them are very unruly and had to be approached carefully.

There were people of all ages from a few months old to people in their eighties living there. The pastors visited them regularly not just for their physical needs, but also for their spiritual needs as well. Each time they went there, people were getting saved, healed and helped. As the number of Christians increased, they started to get bullied and harassed in the camp. Even the pastors were beaten up a few times, but the love of God always compelled all involved, to continue to reach out in love to the least, lost, and marginalised.

We even went in and stood in the unfinished church building, and prayed for the land and for the people. During this time, I remember seeing a shepherd high up on the mountains with a herd of sheep. It reminded me of the *23rd Psalm*. I also thought of Jesus as the good shepherd who had the ninety nine sheep, but still went in search of the one sheep that went astray.

We need to open our eyes to the needs of those around us, and be sensitive to whatever they are going through.

The bible says in: *Philipians 2:5*

> *Let this mind be in you, which was also in Christ Jesus.*

Jesus went about doing good. He came to serve and not to be served. He humbled himself and went to people who were regarded as outcasts in his time. He loved, is still loving and will continue to love, because that is his nature. It is the love of Christ that would compel you, to do the things you would not ordinarily have done, because God is love. If we can embrace the love of God, and what he has already done for us, then we will know that we don't have to strive to be good. We don't have to carry out any rituals to be accepted or loved by God because in:

Romans 5:8 states:

But God demonstrates His own love toward us, in that while we were still sinners, Christ died for us.

All we have to do is be thankful, and enjoy the victorious life that Jesus died to give us. To be able to live and to do this, we just have to accept him as our Lord and saviour.

In the gypsy camp, there were beautiful buildings dotted around. They were owned by corrupt wealthy people around the world, who used these houses to deal drugs, for prostitution and human trafficking. Very sad. The camp was lit up whenever they are around, so they could do their dirty businesses while the others had to stay in darkness and wallow in poverty.

A few weeks before we visited, two young men were electrocuted because they went to tap electricity illegally from the mains nearby. Pastor Stavus and his team however continue to do their best, to solicit help from the government to help them.

We went round some of the huts, handing out food bags and praying for those in need, while the children were having their play sessions with the staff. The need in this camp was huge and it seemed over whelming, but we discovered you just have to have the compassion of Christ, and start from somewhere no matter how little. If we shine the light, others will follow and God will always send help, through his chosen vessels. This was huge food for thought for us all, and when I was asked to lead the devotion the following morning, I shared from:

Mathew 25:35-40

For I was hungry and you gave Me food; I was thirsty and you gave Me drink; I was a stranger and you took Me in; I was naked and you clothed Me; I was sick and you visited Me; I was in prison and you came to Me.

"Then the righteous will answer Him, saying, 'Lord, when did we see You hungry and feed You, or thirsty and give You drink? When did we see You a stranger and take You in, or naked and clothe You Or when did we see You sick, or in prison, and come to You?' And the King will answer and say to them, 'Assuredly, I say to you, inasmuch as you did it to one of the least of these My brethren, you did it to Me."

We will not all go to Athens, but if we look with a heart of compassion, we will see many people in need around us that we can reach out to. Even if it's just a question of saying 'hello,' or running an errand, or giving food or lots of other things. Let's look out for those around us and be a blessing to them, because as the scripture above tells us, we do it unto God. So be it local ministries, charity organisations that support good causes, or people around you, just be a blessing.

CHAPTER 22

MARS HILL

Another highlight to talk about, was going to the Market Square to perform 'The Cupid Shuffle.' If anyone told me I would be dancing in the market square, I would question whether or not they ever knew me! Going to the market with the gospel is what I love to do, but to dance in the market before a big audience, is what I never thought I would ever do, but I did and I loved it.

'Cupid shuffle,' is a dance drama production that tells of the love of Jesus, and how he wants to show us how much he loves us. We are unfortunately often distracted by the things of this world, that profits us nothing. This was the case for a young lady who was involved in a promiscuous life style, addicted to drugs and alcohol and had contemplated taking her own life. When she gave her life to Jesus, she was completely set free. She started a new life in Christ and this new life is available to anyone who would ask for it.

In Romans 10:13; Acts 2:21 it says:
> *For whoever calls on the name of the Lord shall be saved.*

As the dance drama was going on, people were gathering to watch and even join in. Immediately afterwards we dispersed and talked to the people, sharing the gospel with those who were willing to listen. As there were many of them we didn't have enough interpreters to go round. In spite of that however, we still saw many give their lives to the Lord. They were followed up by the Athens Christian Centre, in Ano Patissia. There was much engagement with them, and many seeds were sown in the hearts of the people.

I remember speaking to a Muslim man with another Christian sister. He was very receptive, and after sharing the word of God with him, he told us about how he met some Christians in Egypt, who also told him about Jesus. Apparently at another time in South Africa, he met another group of Christians who also told him about Jesus and gave him a bible. He said he had been reading the bible but didn't quite understand it. We shared the gospel with him once again, and we asked him whether he would like to receive Christ as his Lord and Saviour. He said yes straight away because he was ready.

It goes to show and encourage us all, that we shouldn't worry about what people may say, and whether they will respond or not. Just share your own story and what Jesus has done for you. Leave the rest to the Holy Spirit. Remember, only God gives the increase.

Now my ultimate highlight was climbing the Aeropagus Hill or Mars Hill, where Paul preached to the people of Athens and foreigners about the altar with the inscription: TO THE UNKNOWN GOD. They had built altars for their idol gods and another altar to THE UNKNOWN GOD. They worshipped God without even knowing him.

This was what Paul had to say:

For as I was passing through and considering the objects of your worship, I even found an altar with this inscription: TO THE UNKNOWN GOD. Therefore, the One whom you worship without knowing, Him I proclaim to you: God, who made the world and everything in it, since He is Lord of heaven

and earth, does not dwell in temples made with hands. Nor is
He worshiped with men's hands, as though He needed
anything, since He gives to all life, breath, and all things
Acts 17:23 -25

The moment we pray and ask Jesus to come into our lives, his precious Holy Spirit comes and dwells on the inside of us. So we are the church and wherever we go, Jesus goes because Christ in us, is the hope of all glory. I would love for us to truly get hold of this, and our lives will be changed forever.

Standing on the pinnacle of this hill, and looking at the city of Athens as far as my eyes could see, on this very blustery day made my trip worthwhile. I couldn't help but wonder what the weather was like, when Paul proclaimed Jesus and His resurrection on that hill. Many mocked him then and the story is not much different today. Many however followed him and believed in Jesus Christ.

As followers of Christ, we should always look for opportunities to share the good news of the gospel, and not make assumptions that certain people would not listen or show interest. The world is changing rapidly and many people are perishing or about to, because they lack knowledge or understanding of the word of God. ....*It is not the will of the Father that any should perish.* God has commissioned us to go and tell the story everywhere we go, and he promises to be with us.

Coming back to college and rounding up was very exciting, and for me the third year teachings and practical assignments, were the icing on the cake. Some of the practical assignments made me think of myself differently.

I thought of how far God has brought me, and how all that I've learned will obviously be a blessing to everyone I meet for the rest of my life. This is huge because what the enemy meant for evil, God has turned around for my good, and that will result in my family, friends and everyone I will ever meet, being blessed.

CHAPTER 23

REFLECTIONS AND TESTIMONIES

I stopped and reflected many times on my state of mind when I first started to attend college. Although I thought I was strong, I soon realised how spiritually needful I actually was. I had been so stressed that my hair was falling out, my teeth were chipping for no reason, I had two episodes of shingles and a suspected heart attack. I cried at the slightest thought or remembrance of Charlie, my mother or my niece. As I continued with bible college however, my mind became centred on the finished work of the cross, and the work God has called us to do. This has resulted in my life being transformed and my mind renewed. I know how to take my thoughts captive, and bring them to obedience of Christ.

Proverbs 19:11 states:

> *The discretion of a man makes him slow to anger,*
> *And his glory is to overlook a transgression.*

Our emotions, if not controlled can lead us to several other things like anger, bitterness, resentment, unforgiveness and so on. Also grief with all that comes with it, can lead to some of these issues. So we need to learn to pass over transgressions, offences and the effects of grief.

It is a process, and a journey we have to embark on intentionally. Choose to turn your eyes on to Jesus and learn how to overlook the pain of grief and loss. Choose to worship and enter his rest and the precious Holy Spirit will do the rest. Do I still cry? Yes I do, but now I don't dwell on it long enough, to allow my flesh to take over and cause me to yield to it.

I have discovered so much about myself, and have often wondered when these changes took place in me. Like the chorus of this old hymn says: *turn your eyes upon Jesus, look full in his wonderful face, and the things of earth will grow strangely dim, in the light of his glory and grace*. The change is usually effortless. It is the word of God and the Holy Spirit that does the work.

Most of my time now is spent reading the word and praying. As I stated earlier, I had prayed and asked God to make me like (Anna in the bible). She spent most of her time praying, although she was widowed at a young age. The more I draw close to God, the more I have concluded that to live a victorious life, you have to spend time with God in prayer, study the word and be led by the Holy Spirit.

Life's battles are fought in the place of prayer, not with fists or human words, because we fight not against flesh and blood. Intimacy with God is key to a victorious Christian life because a good idea is not always a God idea! In that place of intimacy however, the will of God and his direction is revealed. He offers us guidance always which is available if we let him lead the way. This will enable us to operate from a position of victory, joy and peace always.

It was during one of my quiet times that the Holy spirit gave me *Isaiah 31:5*. I read the whole chapter including verses 3-5.

Now the Egyptians are men, and not God; And their horses are flesh, and not spirit. When the LORD stretches out His hand,

*Both he who helps will fall, And he who is helped will fall down; They all will perish together. To fight for Mount Zion and for its hill. Like birds flying about, So will the L*ORD *of hosts defend Jerusalem. Defending, He will also deliver it; Passing over, He will preserve it.*

I know that life will be different and sometimes even strange, but the Lord is always with us and whatever comes our way, He will battle for us. This has been my testimony! This is an unfamiliar path but the One who knows the way, has promised to lead us and I know that:

According to *2 Peter3:9:*

The Lord is not slack concerning His promise, as some count slackness, but is longsuffering toward us, not willing that any should perish but that all should come to repentance.

Even when I've made a mistake or taken the wrong move, God is always patient with me and his love always locates me, and brings me back to his presence. God is so faithful and will always honour his word. So much has happened, and the Lord has wrought great victories for my children and I. There is not enough space here for me to mention everything, so I will therefore only mention a few things.

One evening in 2017, my son Ugo was driving back from hospital with his pregnant wife Cynthia. She had gone to get checked out for a minor complaint. Suddenly an inpatient driver cut in front of him, after several failed attempts. When they stopped at the traffic lights, he got out his car, went round to Ugo's car on the driver's side, opened the door, and poured a corrosive liquid all over his face and it went into Ugo's eyes. With his knowledge of chemistry, he knew it was ammonia. It was burning and very painful, so he quickly got out of the car and irrigated his eyes with water. He continued washing his face with water until the police and paramedics came to the scene.

The police had to drive his wife Cynthia back to the house in his car, while the paramedics took him back in an ambulance to the same hospital they had just left, and had been coming from. Despite the fact that the roads were cordoned off and the police searched everywhere, the hooligan escaped.

The testimony is that the attempt to blind and disfigure him by a road raged driver failed! There's not a single scratch on his face, and his eyes are perfect. In fact he went back to work the following day.

His wife Cynthia went on to give birth to a bouncing baby boy who they named after my husband Charlie (Eze). Ezerulamaka Gabriel Osuji arrived on the second anniversary of my mother's call to glory. He was born seven days after his due date, so I knew God brought him out on that day to console me, so I call him my son of consolation, 'Atujuobi,' which also happens to be the name given to me by my paternal grandmother of blessed memory.

In another instance my daughter in law Cynthia, was in severe pain and had to be taken to hospital. She was prepared for an emergency operation because the scan reports showed that she had a ruptured ovarian cyst. This happened in the middle of the funeral ceremony of Bianca's mother's funeral. (Bianca is my second daughter in law). I was meant to be going on my mission trip to Athens in two days. My son Emeka was laid off work about a few weeks before his mother in- law died. Things were tough all round and it was as if the enemy was

was out on a field day trip. One thing was certain however. He had come to the wrong place, and he wasn't welcome and therefore had to be evicted. I began to pray and stood in the gap for my family.

I thank God for Kabod Revival Ministries where people are being discipled and miracles do take place. Out of the blue, my friend who is a co-founder of Kabod Revival ministries, sent me a link inviting me to an online conference called 'Mother's summit.' I keyed into that and began to pray for my family. My prayer partners were also standing with us in prayer.

As the conference was going on, the preacher shared from *Isaiah 61:9* and it states:

> *Their descendants shall be known among the Gentiles, And their offspring among the people. All who see them shall acknowledge them, That they are the posterity whom the* Lord *has blessed.*

Glory to God! I keyed into this scripture and used it to pray for my family, that my seed will be acknowledged for good reports, excellence, promotions, prosperity, victory and so on, because we are already blessed by the Lord.

I carried on declaring this over and over and standing on the word of God, rather than the challenges before us. The funeral ceremony of my daughter in law's mother, went well to the glory of God. We then headed to the hospital to see my other daughter in law before jetting off to Greece. When we arrived at the hospital, things had changed. Cynthia was sent for another scan to confirm the diagnosis before she was wheeled to theatre. She'd had two CT scans already, but they had requested an MRI scan which she'd had in the early hours of that day.

When we saw her, she asked us to start thanking God because she wasn't going to the theatre anymore. "What happened?" we all asked. Apparently the MRI scan showed she had an inflamed appendicitis, and not a ruptured ovarian cyst as previously thought. Another CT scan confirmed that her ovaries were actually fine.

The doctors were surprised and could not explain what had happened. Now was this a misdiagnosis? The answer is No. God intervened and healed her and she was sent home the following day. I was now ready for my mission trip.

My son Emeka shortly after, got a choice job and it has been a place of blessing for him. God provided choice jobs for Uzoma, Ugo, Emeka, Cynthia and Bianca at one time or another. God has been so faithful to us. He never fails. The rocks the enemy threw at us, we used to build an altar of worship to the glory of the Almighty God. Hallelujah!

Grief is a difficult thing to handle and I must say that we all deal with it differently. It makes me wonder when people say, "Don't worry, time will heal." I really don't agree with that statement at all. Time doesn't heal, it is God who heals. If we sweep our emotions under the carpet or compartmentalise them, and expect all the pain and grief to disappear, after a few years, then we've got something else coming. But when we hand over everything to God in that place of prayer, the Holy spirit our comforter will comfort us, and help us to go through it, and come out sane and well.

He will align us with people who will help us during this time, and help us to handle things better. When we do therefore remember our loved ones, we will remember them with joy and thank God for the time we had with them.

This is why one of my most heart-felt pieces of advice I would give, is to cherish what you have, and look after one another. If things are not right, talk it over with people who will be honest with you, and call you to account if need be. See people through God's eyes and love them as He would have us do. My children went through difficult grieving patterns, and we have to understand that everyone is different, and will therefore deal with things in a way that suits them.

At one point, I had to repent and ask God to forgive me for being self-centred. I then called my children together and apologised to them, because I felt I was concentrating more on myself, and not giving them enough attention. Although they didn't think it was the case.

It is the little things that matter so much. Like getting into Charlie's car and going to church, and then us eating out together afterwards. Even the watching of a football match together, as was our family tradition after Sunday service. I miss having Sunday lunch and having football banter about whose team was better. I miss Charlie joking and calling me names like 'Strong Bow,' or 'Bush girl,' and the children roaring with laughter.

It was also time to give parental advise about different things, and offer support where necessary. We did have a wonderful time together as a family, and that is still the case whenever we get together which is fairly often. We have maintained our family prayer times and our monthly fasting, and that has helped us to look after each other and stay strong in the Lord.

I learnt so much from Charlie. He always told me how people judge a man's welfare and happiness by the way his wife is seen outside the home. One of his favourite scriptures to quote about marriage was from:

Proverbs *18:22*

> *He who finds a wife finds a good thing,*
> *And obtains favour from*
> *the LORD.*

Our love was very strong and deep and he spoilt me with lavish gifts. He was also my biggest critic, because he wanted me to be the best I could be.

He was my biggest support in ministry and I also supported him in his also. He had a unique way of interpreting scriptures and he gravitated towards people of like mindedness. His passing created a big void in our lives that only God can fill, and He (God) is helping us to navigate this journey. We haven't arrived yet, but we are on the right path and with GOD on our side, we are winners always. The Husband of the widow and the Father of the fatherless is with us always, and that is more than enough for us.

I had a dream recently about Charlie standing by the window, and calling me to come quickly and have a look at something. I didn't see his face, but it was his build and his voice that called me with a hint of excitement. When I got to the window where he was standing, he was reading some words that were written across the sky. I couldn't see anything but he did, and started reading out the words as follows: "*Behold how good and how pleasant it is in the sight of God.*"

I remember the words were from the book of **Psalm 133** and part of the first verse, so when I woke up, I read the whole of **Psalm 133:1-3**

> *Behold, how good and how pleasant it is For brethren to dwell together in unity! It is like the precious oil upon the head, Running down on the beard, The beard of Aaron, Running down on the edge of his garments. it is like the dew of Hermon, Descending upon the mountains of Zion; For there the LORD commanded the blessing— Life forevermore.*

I know people have said it's not right to dream about a loved one who has passed on for several reasons, but this is different and I truly thank God for being with us, because these past few years have been very challenging.

In this the love of God was manifested toward us, that God has sent His only begotten Son into the world, that we might live through Him.
1 John 4:9

CHAPTER 24

GOD IS OUR REFUGE AND STRENGTH

The enemy has tried to steal, kill and destroy us in many ways, but I thank God for Jesus who came that we might have life and have it to the full. Unity commands blessing and there is strength in unity, and God has kept us and we remain as united as ever.

I have times when I wake up in the night, and I know the Lord wants to talk to me about something or show me something. There are other times when it will just be a time of worship, and thanksgiving to the Lord for his faithfulness. During one such time, I knelt down to pray in the first week of July 2020. The Lord gave me a picture of a hen sitting on a pile of eggs and refusing to move. As I looked on, I felt the Lord tell me that as the hen sits over the eggs, so will the Holy Spirit hover over and incubate us. The fact that we cannot see the eggs does not mean that there's nothing inside the eggs. God is working behind the scenes and in the fullness of time, the chicks will hatch and break free from the shell.

There will be new things unfolding and I certainly look forward to that. God is our shield and protection and will watch over us, as the hen sits over her eggs to protect them. God is with us and I have come to know that life is always a battle between good and evil, but our duty it to stay focused and connected to Christ and we will not be shamed.

1 John 4:9 states:

> *In this the love of God was manifested toward us, that God has sent His only begotten Son into the world, that we might live through Him.*

If we live through Jesus the Son of God, we will not walk in darkness. We will also have nothing to do with the devil, because darkness and light are two parallels that don't mix. As long as we remain in him, we will be victorious in every aspect of life, because it is his will that we should prosper and be in health even as our souls prosper. God has

guided me through these revelations, and with songs during these turbulent years with the COVID-19 virus, and all the malarkey that came with it in 2020. The first song I would like to share is, 'My faith has found a resting place by EE Hewitt and it states:

"My faith has found a resting place, from guilt my soul is freed; I trust the ever living One, his wounds for me shall plead. I need no other argument, I need no other plea, it is enough that Jesus died, and that he died for me. Enough for me that Jesus saves, this ends my fear and doubt; a sinful soul, I come to him, he'll never cast me out. My heart is leaning on the word, the written Word of God, salvation by my saviour's name, salvation through his blood. My great physician heals the sick, the lost he came to save; for me his precious blood he shed, for me his life he gave. I need no other argument, I need no other plea, it is enough that Jesus died and that he died for me."

This hymn says it all for me, and in Christ I have found my rest and He is more than enough for me. It is such a comforting and reassuring song. He is my corner stone and on him alone I build.

I don't know about you but I have always been a praying woman. One of the things I tend to do, is to thank God specially at the end of each year, and seek him concerning the new year. As a result, God has always given me guidance in the form of a word or a picture concerning the coming year.

On the 31st of December 2019, I woke up from sleep singing, "I give myself away," by William McDowell. As I was singing this song and praying a prayer of thanksgiving, the Holy Spirit impressed in my heart: **Psalm 36:9**

For with You is the fountain of life; In Your light we see light.

I began to pray with the words of this Psalm, and ended up reading the whole chapter and was so blessed. We can only see clearly when we look through the eyes of God, and see things the way he sees them. Reflecting on the wording of the song by William McDowell, gave me so much reassurance and hope. It states:

"I give myself away so you can use me. Here I am, here I stand, Lord my life is in your hands. Lord I'm longing to see your desire revealed in me, I give myself away. Take my heart, take my life as a living sacrifice, all my dreams, all my plans Lord, I place them in your hands, I give myself away."

The more I pondered over the Psalm and the song, the more I knew that God wanted me to surrender myself, my family and my ministry to him. This is my confidence, that the Shepherd and Bishop of our souls is asking me to let Him take control of things. All I needed to do was to co-operate with Him and allow Him to lead the way. He never fails and because he said it, I know He will do it.

In February, the Lord gave me a vision of myself and family covered or cocooned in a transparent film. We could see people walking past and everything else happening, but they couldn't see us or touch us. I didn't understand what it meant at first, but after praying I was reassured that whatever happens, God's got us covered and nothing was going to break that seal or covering.

A few weeks later the news of the COVID-19 virus was everywhere, and that resulted in a lot of fear all over most parts of the world. People were dying in high numbers and many stories were being told about the genesis of this virus, and the deadly and devastating impact it was having in our world. So many people lost their jobs, some were furloughed and others were made redundant. Businesses went belly up and life changed, and then of course there was the introduction of the lock down.

Life is about choices. God gave me that vision for a reason, and I had to draw close to the things that matter in life even more. I thank God for men and women of God who were ready to stand up and be counted. They did not consider their lives for the sake of the gospel, and I knew exactly where I needed to be.

In Proverbs 22:3 it states:

> *A prudent man foresees evil and hides himself,*
> *But the simple pass on and are punished.*

It was time to hide but where do we hide? We hide under the shadow of the Almighty, that is our place of safety. When I sensed that the media was propagating fear, I stopped watching the news at the peak of day, so I don't feed my mind with negative things.

Proverbs 4:23 says:

> *Keep your heart with all diligence,*
> *For out of it spring the issues of life.*

What we allow into our minds goes a long way to controlling our thoughts and actions. I needed to guard my heart and ensure my children and grandchildren did the same. We stayed in prayer and with the lockdown now being in full force, and people working from home, it became time for people to rethink about certain things in life. This turned out to be a time of soul searching for many.

I actively and intentionally engaged with the excellent teachings of the word of God by Andrew Wommack Ministries, Your Love world television, Kabod revival ministries and of course my local church, The church at Junction Ten. I didn't want my righteous soul to be vexed, so it was my duty to protect it and take my thoughts captive bringing them into obedience to Christ because as *2nd Corinthians 10:3-4* says:

> *For though we walk in the flesh, we do not war according to the flesh. For the weapons of our warfare are not carnal but mighty in God for pulling down strongholds, casting down arguments and every high thing that exalts itself against the knowledge of God, bringing every thought into captivity to the obedience of Christ.*

Having been in bible college for three years, I'd learnt so much and knew this was action time. One night I woke up singing this chorus, in my native language of Ibo. Later on a friend of mine called me and after our conversation, she asked to pray for my daughter in law who is a frontline member of staff. When we began praying, she quoted the same scripture. Later on that day, the same song that I woke up singing, was posted by a medical doctor in the United States and this song went viral within forty eight hours.

God was telling us that he is with us and we have nothing to be afraid of.

This song is from: *Isaiah 41:10*

> *Fear not, for I am with you; Be not dismayed, for I am your God. I will strengthen you, Yes, I will help you, I will uphold you with My righteous right hand.*

There was no need to fear at all, however my heart was pained, because there were lots of people who didn't know the truth, (that Jesus is the way, the truth and the life). I felt it was my duty to make it known to them that God is in control, and if God be for us then we have nothing to be afraid of!

During this time, although churches and schools and other organisations were in lockdown, we saw a voracious hunger for the word of God. Churches went online and people could stay in their homes, and enjoy several church services in one day. I don't think I had seen Psalm 91 recited, shared, preached as it was during this time. Story had it that the sale of bibles went up by 25%. In one televised broadcast by Your Love World, over 3 billion people tuned in to listen to the word of God, and these programmes went on for months during the lockdown. The result was that millions gave their lives to Jesus. Glory to God.

My local church in their first online broadcast, had thousands listen to the teachings, and many people who left church for one reason or another, started making their way back to church. What the enemy meant for evil, God turned around for good.

My graduation from bible college was via zoom and it didn't take the joy away, except that we couldn't meet physically. In it all I came to realise that lockdown is not a new concept at all. In the bible, Moses was in lock down when he ran away from Pharoah's palace. He was in the desert in the land of the Midianites, and that was when God spoke to him from a burning bush. God spoke to him then about how to deliver the children of Israel from slavery.

Joseph was in lockdown when he was sold into slavery by his brothers, and he ended up in prison for a crime he didn't commit. While in lockdown however, God was preparing him to be the Prime Minister of Egypt.

Samuel was in lockdown, when his mother took him to the temple to serve God under the supervision of Eli the Priest. This was as a fulfilment of her vow to God. When he was sleeping by the Ark of God, the lord appeared to him and spoke to him about the judgement that was to come on the house Eli. He went on to serve God and emerged from lockdown as a king maker, a prophet, a priest and the last Judge of Israel.

What we do when we're in lockdown matters. Although it was a difficult time emotionally, I was very much involved with virtual church activities. This included weekly bible studies with other likeminded Christians in the Father's heart ministry. Also building ourselves up in preparation for the discipleship class, we were about to start before the lockdown was enforced. God put that as a burden in our hearts to disciple the people we met at Bescot market during evangelism.

We have been taking the gospel to this market for ten years, and we have often asked them to look for a good church near them and fellowship there. At the time, we thought we were doing the right thing, until the burden became so heavy on me, that we are bringing them into the kingdom, but leaving them to fend for themselves spiritually.

Although we were discipling the store holders because they are always there whenever we went, but what about the shoppers? It dawned on me that what we were doing wasn't quite right, although we were seeing miracles of salvation, healings, deliverance and so on, we could do better if we could disciple all the new Christians. Jesus called us to make disciples and not to make converts. The Holy Spirit was teaching and preparing us. It has been more or less learning on the job!

When we started ten years ago, we stepped out in faith. We had the passion, and we were willing and available. However we didn't have much experience in evangelism, apart from head knowledge. The Holy Spirit is our teacher and continues to lead the way. It's important that we don't let the flesh get in the way. We have to be 100% dependent on the Holy Spirit.

When I looked back at what we were doing then, I realised that we had been in training by the Holy Spirit and didn't even know, and that was very encouraging. We had made plans to start the discipleship class in the market, when the lockdown was enforced. That left us feeling quite deflated, not knowing how to reach people and our friends in the market.

Paul said in *Galatians 4:19*

> *My little children, for whom I labour in birth*
> *again until Christ is formed in you.*

It's our responsibility to walk alongside them, and invest the kingdom of God in them, pray with and for them until they are able to stand on their own. We are to be the support they need, so the enemy will not snatch them away. I would liken it to giving birth to a baby and

leaving them to fend for themselves. Something was wrong here.

We carried on praying and interceding about this, and the Holy Spirit gave us wisdom, and guidance and aligned us with people that worked with us. We had to think outside the box, since we were not allowed to physically go to the market. Also because of the restrictions and changes that came with Covid-19, including social distancing, hand gelling and masks. The Holy Spirit impressed it on my heart that we needed to do something quickly. We therefore acquired a phone, and printed some contact cards with bible verses and a phone number.

We did all these things as we waited for the time when the lock down restrictions would be lifted. When it happened, we restarted again and this time, we were not putting up tables with materials like books and leaflets. We didn't interact with them as we use to do, but we now went round the market and interacted with them, offering them pastoral support and praying for them. Since then we have seen some tremendous miracles and a real shift in the spirit realm.

It was during this time that we met a lady I call Miss V. She is our Samaritan woman, our person of peace. The day we met her, she didn't want to engage with us initially, but when we offered to pray for her, she consented because she said she had a lot of 'enemies.' While another sister was praying for her, God gave me a word for her. It was that as she focused on God he would take care of the rest. When I shared this with her, it resonated with her straight away. We then carried on and saw other people.

Two weeks later she was looking for us everywhere. Apparently, on the day we prayed for her, she sold nearly all of her goods, and then not much happened after that. She couldn't find the card that we had given her, so she had not been able to contact us. When she did eventually manage to, she testified about what happened the day we met her. She then asked us to pray for healing, and favour from her customers. I prayed with her over the phone, and after a few days, she called and gave a testimony of healing and many sales.

This pattern has continued and it was a welcome one for us, as we were able to offer prayer support and pastoral care over the phone. The more we prayed for her, the more she came back with testimonies. She has been spreading the word to other people, and referring them for prayers. The phone can get busy sometimes with requests and that's exciting for us.

Now Miss V went to a function and one of the organisers fell and hurt her shoulder. Miss V prayed for her and then called me to pray for the lady again. When she got me on the line, I heard the lady telling her she shouldn't have called me, because when she prayed for her, the pain left her!

She's not just referring people to us, she now prays for them also. Miss V has gone from laying her goods on the floor, to being able to afford payment for a table to lay her goods. She is now sourcing goods directly from factories, and she makes many sales each time.

That's not all! She also has a second job as a cleaner, to help her make ends meet. She had increased her hours and she would be taking up a supervisory role in the same company, where a few months ago she was accused of something she didn't do. After we prayed, God exonerated her and has blessed her. Now she is a blessing to others.

She has joined our teleconference discipleship class, which started a few months ago. God is awesome. There are lots of testimonies from the market place, and I consider myself to be so privileged to be out there with the team, sharing the love of Jesus Christ and to see miracles take place. Glory to God!

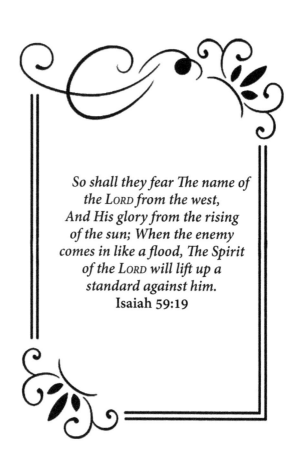

So shall they fear The name of the LORD from the west, And His glory from the rising of the sun; When the enemy comes in like a flood, The Spirit of the LORD will lift up a standard against him.
Isaiah 59:19

CHAPTER 25

EBENEZER

Having retired from the National Health Service (NHS) as a Community Matron in Jan 2019, I feel so happy that I left the NHS when I did, especially in the wake of COVID-19 and all the problems that have come with it. I heard from the Lord and I am so much at peace. I didn't retire because I was unhappy, but because I knew it was time to explore the things I've always wanted to do in life. Besides I didn't want to look back and regret not leaving, when I knew the Holy Spirit was prompting me to do so.

When I tell people I was in bible college, the questions are usually what are you training to be? A pastor? The answer is that I went into bible college to fulfil the dream I shared with Charlie. It was to study and learn more about God. Now that I have finished, I dedicate every resulting fruit, to the memory of my late husband. Wherever that success story takes me, his name will always be mentioned, and I know he is looking down and smiling in appreciation and pride.

I know God has plans for me and he will allow them to unfold in his time. In the mean-time I devote my time to the ministries, and my local church, who have supported my children and I in prayer all these years. Kabod Revival Ministry is a safe place for me, and I always join other generals of God in intercession for the world, people in need, nations and our families, and whatever else God lays on our hearts to pray for.

When my heart is troubled or I have a burden in my heart, I usually can't wait for the next session, to connect and be in that place of prayer. It has provided the space for me to rest, and the opportunity that I asked of God, to make me like Anna.

Kabod is a place of opportunities and discipleship. This was the vision of two sisters. One is a practicing GP and the other a practicing Lawyer. It started with less than 10 people a few years ago, and now it has grown to almost 400 members. It has reassured me that you can disciple, and hold studies over the phone, via free conference calls or zoom apps and still continue to grow. The only times we physically met were during our May, July and December retreats.

I have volunteered to help other students and the Ministry of Andrew Wommack, because I went into Charis Bible College a very grief stricken and broken woman, and came out victorious in every aspect of life. My victory was not because of the school, but because of the teaching, learning and coaching that is offered to students and staff. The least I can do now is to sow back into the ministry, where I discovered a lot about myself and so much more about God!

We are blessed to be a blessing. Since my third year in CBC till now, I have become more involved with my local church, the Church at Junction Ten. This is an Assemblies of God Church, and it's fully committed and aligned to the church values we have and believe in, as well as that of the AOG worldwide. I love serving and helping out wherever I can.

As the leader of 'Father's Heart Ministries,' which is one of the missional teams in my church, I will continue to reach out to the least, the lost and the marginalised, until God says otherwise. I will use the rest of my days to serve God, who has kept my children and I, bringing us this far. He calls me friend and has invited me for a walk. I'm in his hands to stay, till he calls me home.

The Lord has blessed us with two more grandchildren since my husband Charlie went to be with the Lord. Our quiver is filling up very quickly and I'm still counting, by God's special grace. All through the storms, the love of God has been an anchor to our souls. He has revealed himself to us in different ways, all throughout this time. He is our **father, friend, saviour, healer, guardian, master, my husband** and so on. He is My Jehovah El-Roi, (The God who sees me) and because he is with us, we will always win!

My children are well established in their chosen fields and they are doing very well. My grandchildren have been a great source of joy to me, and every day I see Charlie in all of them, through their personalities, words, mannerisms, sense of humour and views on things generally. Through them, he is very much alive in my heart! They don't however always have his dress sense which was impeccable by the way.

God has continued to guide me through his eyes, so my duty is to stay focused on him alone. It has made me realise even more, that life without Christ is empty and meaningless. I always remember the word he gave me for this year:

For with You is the fountain of life; In Your light we see light.
Psalm 36:9

I would rather look through Christ than through my natural eyes. This is what I teach my children and grandchildren, to always see things God's way, for his ways are different from the ways of man. When we see things his way, we act circumspectly and redeem time and then always win. It hasn't been an easy journey, but it has been a very victorious one because of HIM who leads the way.

> *I have heard of You by the hearing of the ear,*
> *But now my eye sees You.*
> Job 42:5

When you're eyes see the Lord in your circumstances, no matter what that might be, your story will change. I have known him all my life, but now I know him in a different way. I can assure you that there is no other way for me and mine. Charlie has gone to glory, and I have the responsibility of being mother and father at the same time. I can also assure you that, this is not an easy responsibility. The things I would have shared with Charlie, I now have to figure out myself, with the help of the Holy Spirit. I tell him everything. I have always been someone who is private, especially with my thoughts. I mull things over before I make decisions, but since I lost Charlie and my mother, I have learned to off load on my children. I tend to bore them with my views and decisions, whether they take it in or not. I have learned to open up a lot more to them. They are my friends and confidants and they've been brilliant.

One of the scriptures that God gave me, which I have had to revisit over and over is from:

> *I will bring the blind by a way they did not know; I will lead*
> *them in paths they have not known. I will make darkness*
> *light before them, And crooked places straight.*

These things I will do for them, And not forsake them.
Isaiah 42:16

The day God gave me this scripture, my heart leapt because this is an unfamiliar path for me, I really do not know how to wear these big shoes I've been left to wear by my husband and mother. I can never have another mother, neither will ever have another Charlie (Eze) as I fondly call him, BUT I have God who has promised to show me how to navigate life from now on.

This makes me a winner, because the master of the universe is showing me the way. He will cause all the darkness around me to spring forth into light, and rugged roads to be made straight and that's not all. He promises never to leave or forsake me. That for me is awesome because Christ in me, is the hope of all glory. When I feel pain, lonely or I become teary for one reason or another, I recite my favourite **Psalm 121** and I turn to Jesus.

When I become bored which is not very often, I pack up a suitcase and go off to see my children and my four beautiful grandchildren. They keep me occupied and I get to play with them, which is fun although it leaves my body aching sometimes. I wouldn't however swap it for anything in this world. They are very special and I know most grandparents say the same thing, but honestly my grandchildren are special.

Isaiah 59:19 states:

> So shall they fear The name of the LORD from the west, And His glory from the rising of the sun; When the enemy comes in like a flood, The Spirit of the LORD will lift up a standard against him.

The enemy truly came in like a flood, but I thank God for Jesus. He has already fought the battle and defeated Satan, so although my loved ones are no longer here, I will see them again because we don't grieve like them that have no hope. I will see them again because they ran their race and finished well. It's now up to me to align myself to the things of God, and be in right standing with the Lord, so I too will also finish well. The Lord is guiding us and teaching us every step of the way.

The Lord has continued to raise a higher standard for us. I have also hung on to *Job 14:7-9* that states:

> *For there is hope for a tree, If it is cut down, that it will sprout again, And that its tender shoots will not cease. Though its root may grow old in the earth, And its stump may die in the ground, Yet at the scent of water it will bud And bring branches like a plant.*

We may have been hit by the storms of life, but I thank God that we have an anchor that keeps our souls safe and secure. The tender branches will not cease, and God is making an oak tree out of us. I thank God for the life I shared with Charlie. He was the best, and is still the love of my life and will never be forgotten. He has left me replicas of him to remember him by. God is restoring my family and he will continue to lead us victoriously all our days. Jesus is Lord!

I will round up with a story of the children of Israel as documented in: *1 Samuel 7:7-17*

> *But the LORD thundered with a loud thunder upon the Philistines that day, and so confused them that they were overcome before Israel. Then Samuel took a stone and set it up between Mizpah and Shen, and called its name Ebenezer, saying, "Thus far the LORD has helped us."*

It's a long read, so I paraphrased it, but please look it up yourself and see how God wrought great victory for Israel. Israel was surrounded by enemies that pestered and threatened them and they went to Samuel, (who was the Judge and Priest in Israel at the time). They cried unto him not to stop crying to God on their behalf, to save them from the hands of the philistines. As it was the practice in those days, Samuel took a suckling lamb and offered it to God as a burnt sacrifice wholly unto the Lord. While he was offering up this sacrifice, the philistines drew near to battle against Israel.

Now the outcome of this was that the Philistines were subdued, Israel took their cities back from the Philistines. God delivered Israel and there was peace between Israel and her neighbours. God gave them great victory. The name Ebenezer has also meant so much to us, because at every stage in our lives, God has always fought for us and given us victory.

At some point there was a project we did some years back that we were planning to name Ebenezer. Also during our 25th wedding anniversary, our then senior pastor and the (founder of our church Pastor John Price), preached from this portion of scripture without knowing it's significance to us.

I have shared only a little bit of what God has done for my family and I. God has fought and continues to fight our battles for us, and has always given us victory. I don't know what you are going through in

your life and what challenges you face. Human beings change, seasons change and so do our circumstances, but

God never changes and his mercies never fail. As he fought for the children of Israel, discomfited their enemies and wrought great victory for them, so will he do the same for you. You only need to call upon him and he will surely answer you and give you victory in your situation.

I married a wonderful man, a very special person, a rare gem, the love of my life who loved me for who I was. He was a straight talker and fearless in many ways. He hated injustice and stood up for the oppressed. He was a voice to the voiceless. He loved God and lived an accomplished life. He gave me three beautiful replicas of him, and other replicas coming from them too. He's handed the baton to me, and I will not fall by God's grace. I thank God for Jesus and because he lives, we will live also, and this is how far he has helped us. This is my Ebenezer!

ABOUT THE AUTHOR

Chidinma U. Osuji a devout Christian, with a unique passion for evangelism especially in the marketplace, still takes the gospel of Jesus Christ to the least, the lost and the marginalised.

She is also a retired Nurse, a Charis Bible college graduate, a mother and grandmother who loves to cook for her family and friends. Chidi the widow of late Dr Ezerulamaka Charles Osuji, has turned life around with God's help, and lives in the United Kingdom with her family.

*D*ear reader/writer,

I would like to take this opportunity to thank you for supporting one of our newest authors.

Here at Open Scroll Publications, we specialise in assisting talented writers to fulfil their dreams and aspirations. The creative process is hard enough as it is without having to worry about getting your masterpiece published once you're finally done. That's why Open Scroll Publications was formed. We demystify the process of getting published, and give a literary voice to those who would otherwise be muted in obscurity.

Our list of gifted writers is rapidly growing, and I would like to invite you to consider becoming our next distinguished author. So, whether you're working on a novel, a children's book, a poetry anthology, or an inspirational non-fiction piece, why not take a leap of faith and contact us? We would love to hear from you.

For more information, please visit us at:
www.openscroll.co.uk
info@openscroll.co.uk
Phone: 01213502422
       07506677504

Or write to us at:
Open Scroll Publications Ltd,
Kemp House,
160 City Road,
London, EC1V 2NX.